THEOLOGICAL APPROACHES TO
PASTORAL CARE

Is Anybody Listening?

MARTIN L. JOHNSON

ISBN: 978-1-957009-62-9 (sc)

Library of Congress Control Number: 2022916200

Table of Contents

DEDICATION

To Aldoro and Gabriel Johnson, my parents whose faith, hope, and love saw our family through the crises of childhood, introduced me to Jesus Christ, the Chief Care Giver, and brought me thus far on my way.

To the patients at Walter Reed Army Medical Center, Washington, D.C., whose sickness provided an opportunity for ministry. To the medical staff and members of the Interdisciplinary Team who tolerated my following them around while performing surgery and other medical functions. A special note of thanks goes to the pathologists who demonstrate through autopsies how what God has created can be dissected to determine causes of human ills and death. To the thousands of soldiers and family members whose needs for healing met with my needs as a wounded healer. These are the true heroes and heroines of faith and authors of this book.

ACKNOWLEDGMENTS

This book was born, nurtured and brought to fruition as a result of crises. There are many people who were a part of this project. My Clinical Pastoral Care supervisor who took what I brought to him and molded out of him a caring pastor; the librarians at Walter Reed Army Medical Center and at the U.S. Army Chaplains School who did much of the work in locating pertinent materials for the project; to my family, much of whose time owed to them was taken away while writing this book; to Mrs. Willa Mae Harris, a dedicated customer and supporter of whatever I write; to Mrs. Cathy McAphee, my secretary, who learned how to use our new computer during this project; and to the Mt. Olive Church Family, the boldest people in the world, who trust me to give them the Words of eternal life. May God richly reward them for their patience and endurance. Hopefully reading this book will be as helpful as sitting through a one-hour sermon from which you get essentially nothing; of existential value, if you sit through it, at least you will have learned a lesson in patience. God bless!!

INTRODUCTION

To the Churches of Galatia Paul writes these words: "God sent His Son, born of a woman, born under the law...", (Galatians 4:4). What Paul is suggesting is that the event of the ages, the fulfillment of prophetic predictions and the culmination of the long wait for the divine promise of salvation have arrived. Theologically and historically. The advent of Jesus Christ was orchestrated by the divine time clock. Jesus was not bore a minute early nor a minute late; rather, he was born at the right time, the only time he could have been born. Paul seeks to make this very clear in his usage of the Greek vocabulary at the point where lie deliberately uses the word chronos (clock time) as opposed to the word kairos (the only time). But in the letter that Paul writes to the church at Rome, he states: "For when we were yet without Strength, in due time (kairos, the right time) Christ died for the ungodly." What the Apostle Paul wishes us to know here is that Christ was both an historical personality and a divine being. The advent of the Christ of God revealed in human flesh set in motion a spiritual dynamic with far-reaching implications for Christian ministries. The essence of that dynamic is captured within the confines of the theologies set forth in both the Old Testament Scriptures and in a number of New Testament letters. The primary focus of Jesus' ministry was/is total liberation from systems, ideologies, and sins that seek to render persons less than totally free human beings.

The essence of that dynamic is captured within the confines of the theologies in the Scriptures. The Human predicament, whatever that means, is not beyond the reach and rescue of the Christ of God. To assist humanity to rid themselves of the failures, hurts, ills, fears, evils and sins that impede wholeness and total personhood, Clinical Pastoral Education (CPE) is offered as an approach to ministry that helps to enhance health, happiness, coping, restoration and wholeness.

The Church of God in Christ stands at a significant crossroad in her relatively new, rich, and glorious earthly pilgrimage; and, as it is with other earthly and historical organizations, the church is faced with the colossal task of providing quality spiritual ministries to a hurting and broken humanity. "The basis and norm for Christian ministry must be the message of the historical Jesus as is located in the New Testament Scriptures. In addition to taking advantage of the power and resources of Scripture, there is available to us a number of social and secular resources, that have proven growth-enhancing for persons who reflect both the medical and spiritual perspectives. Clinical Pastoral Education is one such professional approach to the healing process. The degree of spiritual and theological preparation, coupled with genuine commitment, determine the effectiveness of ministry.

The experience gained at Walter Reed Army Medical Center in Washington, D.C., while serving as a senior United States Army Chaplain, provided for me a large list of approaches to ministry. These approaches might also prove to the reader to be ministry-enhancing. Christian ministry must have a strong theological base! There must be a reason for what one does in ministry. The writer has attempted to explained what seem to be biblical, and theological bases upon which effective ministry is provided.

Human hurt and brokenness effect Church of God in Christ parishioners of all ages, gender, socio-economic statuses, and levels of academic achievements. Let me suggest that within the confines of the Word of God is found the answers and the resolutions to all human hurts and ills: spiritual, emotional and mental, to mention a few. Therefore, it is significant for us to know that caregivers are called upon by the time in which we live to be viable witnesses to the love and grace of God, regardless of the individual sins, or sinners to whom we find occasions to minister. My prayer is that the readers' intellectual and ministerial repertoires are enhanced by the theological insights shared in this short volume. Remember the key to becoming an effective minister of God's Word is to remain in the state of becoming.

CHAPTER I

THEOLOGICAL BASES FOR ACTIVE LISTENING IN THE DELIVERY OF PASTORAL CAR

The message of Jesus is at least twofold. On the one hand it is steriological, and on the other hand it is eschatological. It is stereological in the sense that it is a message of hope, help and wholeness in this world and beyond. It is eschatological in the sense that it offers an end to the present situation of a broken. Disjointed and hurting world. The message of the earthly Jesus offers this futuristic hope while, at the same time, maintaining the value of this present life. This is the meaning of St. John's report of Jesus: "I am come that you might have life wore abundantly..." The message of the Jesus of history is located in the books that historically comprise the Synoptic Gospels and the Fourth Gospel, and in a significant portion of the teachings of Jesus as they are quoted in a number of the Pauline letters, found in the New Testament. The message of Jesus is the presupposition for the theologies of the New Testament rather than a part of the theologies contained therein. The kerygma or the proclamation of the historical Jesus thus becomes the basis of and the point of" departure for Christian theology. It is in that sense that the writers of the Gospels and of the Epistles of the Early Church gave to the earliest Christian community their understandings of the message of Jesus. The early theologians had at their disposal their personal observations of, and their experiences with Jesus; and, of course, the oral traditions of the community as primary source materials.

The primary function and responsibility of those persons who are engaged in the pastoral ministry is to facilitate the healing process that leads to wholeness of persons. Whatever else the activities and ceremonies in which ministers find themselves, the primary call and function should always be kept in focus. It seems to me that a definition of Jesus' total ministry is captured in the words: wholeness, completeness, and restoration. I shall not be so presumptuous as to assume that this book will be exhaustive in defining wholeness, completeness and restoration; however, I shall not use that as an excuse to dismiss these foci as indefinable and unreachable in word and practice. There are hundreds and literally thousands of people engaged in the Pastoral ministry who find themselves backed up against a wall of apparent impossibility where they are faced with situations and issues in ministry to which they have no answer, and over which they have no control. Each occasion for ministry is perhaps unique and different; each suffering. Hurting and broken person's situation presents a new or different set of needs and concerns, and each need and concern might necessitate a different answer and resolution.

The needs, desires, and expectations of each broken person will depend largely upon a multiplicity of data: social, cultural, religious, racial, ethnic, economic, and even educational. What I perceive as a tragedy in Pastoral ministry is the same as is true in Religious Education: those who desire mostly to participate are most deficient in their preparation. In my own religious tradition, the emphases placed upon training in theological education is relatively recent. While the four basic functions of Pastoral Care were very much a part of my tradition, there was not much effort to set them to written form or put them in a book. The practice of Pastoral Care occurred separate and apart from any conscious theological sophistication as determined by a council.

The black religious experience in America is a most vivid example of Pastoral Care in action: healing, sustaining, guiding, and reconciling. While this book is not an examination of nor an evaluation of the black religious experience, it helps me in my Pastoral ministry to draw upon the rich resources of my racial and religious heritage and tradition. The purpose of this little book is to examine the biblical records for situations and opportunities where Pastoral Care occurred, and where the caregivers, through active listening, were facilitative in the Pastoral functions. The major emphasis of the book will be upon the hearing of what was said verbally and non-verbally, and based upon what was actually communicated, Pastoral Care occurred. I shall attempt to point out a number of theological norms, bases and examples for active listening as a prerequisite to a more effective delivery of Pastoral Care. While I might positively exploit a number of tasks, skills and insights made available to me by other academic disciplines. As a minister of the word and sacrament, I am primarily a "sometime" theologian. To have available to me in a concise and relatively condensed form a theological analysis of biblical passages and situations in which active listening and hearing inevitably preceded Pastoral Care could further sensitize we to the significance of hearing, and thus enhance the effectiveness of the delivery of Pastoral Care.

1. DEFINITIONS OF THEOLOGY

Theological definitions are as varied and are as numerous as there are theologians. The content and character of a theology is essentially reflective of the socio-cultural and religious in milieu out of which the theologian emerges. John Macquarrie in his book, <u>Principles of Christian Theology,</u> suggests a basic function of the theologian and of the theology espoused as being "Loyal to the faith he seeks to express and relevant to the community it seeks to address." While this definition suggests loyalty and relevancy, James Cone in his book, <u>A Black Theology of Liberation,</u> defines theology ". . . as a rational study of the being of God in the world in the light of the existential situation of an oppressed community". Rudolph Bultmann is of the position that "...theology is the explication of both the implicit and explicit message of the New Testament". Seward Hiltner in his book, Theological Dynamics, defines theology as a *... reflective and implicative enterprise that might or might not be religious". 'While Hiltner suggests that religion is not necessarily theology, he concludes that the consequences of theology transcend the parameters of religion. The definitions of theology are varied and numerous and will depend largely upon the perspectives of the theologians. I, as a "sometime" theologian, am a part of a religious community that has provided me with a rich heritage and with a strong religious tradition upon which I can draw for a definition of theology. Theology for me is a human attempt (under the unction of the Holy Spirit) to talk about, to understand and to interpret the activities of the beyond-the-human and relate their meanings to the existential situations of people. Therefore, for me, theology is not merely God-talk or just talk about God, but it is to understand what God weans to the whole of life now. For instance: What does the message of the Jesus of history that was spoken 2000-years ago have to say to me and to my situation Today?

A. Euro-American Theology

The total focus, aim, and ultimate goal of theology is to allow the message of Jesus to provide relevance and meaning to the intended audience. That message is to bring total liberation from all of the social, political, economic, religious and evil systems which seek to dehumanize, depersonalize, demoralize, disenfranchise, demean and render the person less than a complete and whole person in this world. The theologian is both a theologian and a philosopher. As a theologian, the function is that of an exegete, or one who explicates, elucidates and makes the message relevant. This task requires the use of the most coherent and understandable language available. A basic presupposition is that there is a message of hope and doom located in the word of God. As a philosopher, the function is not only be to a lover of truth and wisdom, but to raise questions that lead those who would be lovers of truth and wisdom to that truth and wisdom which is sometimes concealed in life.'

Theology, its role and function, depends largely upon the religio-cultural perspective of the theologian. The definition of theology that has as its core liberation is a rather safe definition if you are referring to Black and Third- World theologians, but to have the audacity to suggest that liberation is the core of all theologies is a false assumption, if by liberation you mean freedom from the socio-political and economic systems that tend to render man less than a total person. It seems quite significant to me, as a person of the twentieth-century, that during the eighteenth century the Bishop of London saw no inconsistency between slavery and Christianity. Therefore, a slave-holder could be both a slave-holder and a Christian simultaneously and fail to come under any condemnation of the church or the Wrath of God as interpreted by a number of white theologians but the Bishop was not alone in his theological position, a large number of American church leaders also justified slavery by reading into both Old and New Testament passages what they promoted as God-ordained second class human beings.

It would be unfair to suggest that all white theologians and church leaders were pro-slavery, just as it would be unfair to suggest that all of them were anti-slavery, but the pro-slavery group seemed much larger than the latter.

Let me raise the question as to what do the theologies of Karl Barth, Rudolph Bultman, John Calvin, Martin Luther and Paul Tillich mean to a poor black man whose skills are minus the academic and intellectual sophistication that are traditionally a prerequisite to the understanding of those systems? It seems to me that a relevant question is what do the councils of Trent, Nicaea, and Chalcedon mean to a poor, sick, and hurting white or black person whose life and future are suddenly being altered by some contagious, incurable disease? It seems to me that the answers to these ultimate questions lie within the confines of God's Word rather than in some esoteric theologies that are formulated apart from the situation they seek to address. It seems to me that the ongoing task of theologians to explore the biblical records, human experiences and the human predicament to provide solutions and answers to the existential problems and questions which plague humanity, such as war, poverty, hunger, disease, human hurt, racism, sexism and to other concerns we experience in this world in which we live and move and strive to live out our personhood.

Euro-American, White Anglo-Saxon Protestant theologians have historically, systematically, and systemically done theology from their perspective and have sought to impose their results and conclusions upon blacks and other minorities without seeking input from them nor the experiences of other and varied perspectives. What the preceding statement means is that the so-called dominant culture assumes to have an understanding of the needs of another's culture and religious experience without asking, and without that input, they proceed to suggest an across-the-board application. This, to me, is an approach that is foreign to the task of theology and is tantamount to the minister offering to be with the patient without ever finding out the location of the patient.

That approach suggests arrogance, presumptuousness, and superiority that get in the way of ministry. The Pastoral Caregiver who readily understands and accepts the given of varieties of backgrounds and perspectives and the impact they have upon those whom he seeks to serve will find active listening an indispensable tool as one seeks to identify needs. It seems impossible to me for one to be able to meet a need without first ascertaining and identifying the need.

The basic stigma that is inevitably associated with a significant portion of Euro-American theology is that theologians completely disregarded, ignored and over-looked a significant segment of the human community: Blacks, Hispanics, and Third-World peoples because these peoples were not a part of the listening agenda of the theologian. Therefore, the persons in real need of help were not heard, their needs were unidentified, and how does one help without knowing where help is needed? It seems to me that this is the core of James Cone's argument in his book, <u>God of the Oppressed:</u>

"In order for the theologian to recognize the particularity of black religion, the theologian must imagine his/her way into the environment and the ethos of black slaves ... who had to feel their way along the course of American slavery... while still affirming their humanity."

This quote, while referring specifically to the failure of the so-called mainline theologians to take seriously another vital human experience and address accordingly, also has significance for the caregiver. There is the need to empathize and put yourself into the world of the sick and hurting and really hear what is being said and responding accordingly.

B. Concepts of Black Theology

Black theology, or the theology that emerges from the experiences of black people whose lives have been reduced to mere chattel slavery, is the direct results of the failure of Euro-American WASP (White Anglo-Saxon Protestant) theology to take seriously the plight of the oppressed. This does not suggest, however, that all WASP were pro-slaver or anti-minority for there were large numbers of non-blacks who dared to speak out against a slave mentality, many of whom were white southern preachers. Nonetheless, the theological scholarship of Europe and America has not spoken directly to the existential situation of an oppressed community. But Black theology, not unlike the "God is-dead concept", has gotten the attention of the larger segment of the world's religious community. While I was equally startled, as were many in the religious community. Upon hearing of God's death, brit after having examined certain concepts of God harbored by many, I later concurred that the god of their perception should die and 1 would deliver the eulogy, free of charge. The God who takes the side of the powerful against the weak must be a racist. The god of the white slave master cannot possibly be the same god of the slave. Major Jones was right "...whites derived their right to rule over blacks from God." Care-givers who happen to be white, black or representatives of other ethnic minorities would do well to keep in mind the influence and power of cultural history when engaging themselves in the Pastoral ministry.

Black theology is black folks talking about God and how He relates to them in their own peculiar and particular situations. Black theology occurs when black theologians, sometimes theologians, black intellectuals, the uneducated, the jobless, the homeless, and the bums in the alleys and gutters of our society attempt to bring some sanity and meaning to a complex, inconsistent, unjust world in which "...we live and move and have our being." Black theology is the response to the Euro-American care-giver who did not bother to ask me where I hurt nor how I feel, but assumed that he already knew and offered me what his history and culture told him I needed. Black theology is a protest against that sin of arrogance and it is a bold statement, which says that I am of age and that I am capable of speaking for myself. Black theology is both the verbal and affective response of a sick, injured, and hurting patient who is insisting that the minister talks less and listens more. It is the patient who says my smile is misleading and if you would only look at me and listen to me you could really hear what I am saying Black theology seeks to do essentially what Jesus, the Pastoral caregiver does in Mark's Gospel, 5: 1-9, 15, where Jesus exercises the demons in his encounter with the Gadarene demoniac. Jesus was able to look beyond the presenting accolades and see the real need of the person and confronts him by asking him his name. His name was a question of identity. Jesus knew that if he could get the man to say who he thought he was, then Jesus could commence helping identify who he really was. It is rather strange that in verse 15 where, after a positive encounter with Jesus, the man's total persona is changed, he is now clothes and sitting at Jesus' feet.

But what is so strange is that now those who see him with his changed personality are now afraid. Noticeably, no one is afraid of him while he is in the cemetery with a strange hairdo, weird clothes on, and low britches on; but as soon as he is educated and has some clothes on and is in his right mind, they are afraid. Black theology is about helping black folk's identity who they really are, putting on clothes and sitting at the feet of teachers until they are prepared to enter the world of work and alter their economic conditions. It might be that people who have always kept you back will now become afraid of you, or give you the attention, jobs, and opportunities heretofore denied.

Black theology, as is Euro-American theology, is Christian theology in the sense that the biblical record is its basic source with Jesus Christ as the norm. However, Black theology differs from Euro-American theology in the sense that the black experiences also serve as a primary source of the theology espoused. A basic presupposition of the theological enterprise is that God is understood within the context of cultural and existential experiences and that His acts are expressed via the symbols and signs familiar to the receiving cultural community. Therefore, Black theology is Christo-centric, biblically based and is attuned to the relevant and pertinent questions raised, and needs expressed by the primary community it seeks to serve. That, to me, seems to be the primary point of departure of Christian theology.

C. A Colorless Theology

The relatively recent re-emergence-although one cannot forget David Walker, fat Turner, Harriett Tubman and Henry High land Garnet- and rise (1950's and 60's) of modern day Black Theology has come under constant and frequent attack by the so-called mainstream theologians.

Very few theologians, if any had ever given any thought to theology so far as color was concerned, prior to the 1950's and 60's. After all, theology was done in the Ivory Tower by Ivy League thinkers and, without question, it was white, and white was tantamount to being right. H. Richard Niebuhr suggests that the color line drawn between churches was based upon theology rather than social realities.' I find it quite difficult to believe that it was either or rather than both and the same. For one's socio-cultural milieu determines largely one's thought processes. It is rather unfortunate that white American theology from Cotton Mather, Jonathan Edwards, Reinhold Niebuhr and even to Schubert Ogden has interpreted the message of Jesus within the socio-economic and political interest of white people without much regard for people of color.

The validity, credibility, and integrity of white theology enjoyed a long and flourishing history until the rise of modern black theologians in the 1950's and 60's. The 50's and 60's gave rise to a wore formalized expression of what blacks thought and felt regarding their deplorable conditions in America. Black theology is the black religious community's expression of their understanding of the God who is their constant help. But Since the rise of a more formalized expression of black concern, the white theological community has begun to question the validity of a black theology. The question has to do with the color of the theology. Black theology does not literally wean color: Black, White, Red, Brown, etc.

However, color is synonymous with need, hearing, relevance and meaning. Black theology is a result of reading the same biblical texts that the slave master read to justify slavery and hearing a totally different message. Therefore, to suggest a colorless theology is to negate and deny peoples of color the right to appropriate to the black situation the first-century message of Jesus in these "last and evil days".

The theology of traditional America has failed to raise the existential question that answers the dilemma of a poor and dehumanized minority of black Americans. The question has to do with the meaning of the message of Jesus for individual freedom, justice and equality in this world and the world to come. Theology is not therefore one-dimensional, nor is it primarily other-worldly; rather, theology must deal with the totality of human existence. Theology is existential when its answers speak to the howness of existence, rather than to the abstract and remote past and futuristic possibilities of humanity.

1   John Macquarrie. Principles of Christian Theology. (New York: Charles Scribners' Sons, 1966), p.2.
2   James Cone. A Black Theology of Liberation. (New York: J. B. Lippencott Company, 1970), p. 17.
3   Rudolph Bultmann. The Theology of the New Testament. (New York: Charles Scribners' Sons, 1955), p. 26.
4   Seward Hiltner. Theological Dynamics. (Nashville: Abingdon Press, 1972), p. 185.
5   James Cone. God of the Oppressed. (New York: The Seabury Press, 1975), pp. 8-10.
6   Carter G. Woodson. The Negro Church in History (Washington, D.C.: The Associated Publishers, Inc., 1922), pp. 61-70.
7   Clement Eaton. The Freedom-of-Thought Struggle in the Old South. (New York: Harper & Row, 1964), pp. 290-292.
8   James Cone. God of the Oppressed (New York: The Seabury Press, 1975), pp. 10-11.

9   Major J. Jones. <u>Christian Ethics for Black Theology.</u> (Nashville: Abingdon Press, 1974), pp. 88-89.

10   H. Richard Niebuhr. Christ and Culture (New York: Harper & Row, 1951), Chapter IX.

CHAPTER II

WHAT LISTENING IS

The ability to not only listen but to hear is significant to a helping relationship. The patient who at age thirty has just been told that his open-heart surgery has rendered him unfit for military service and that lie is to be mandatorily retired, responds with a firm laugh as if nothing has happened, might be sending false messages. If the caregiver listens and facilitates in a caring manner, there might emerge the gut-level feelings, thus allowing the real to be treated. For Pastoral Care to be given, hearing is indispensable. For hearing to occur. The listener must listen beyond the verbal and listen for the affective non-verbal. Therefore, active listening is an inevitable prerequisite to the delivery of effective Pastoral Care.

Carl Rogers in his book, Encounter Groups, points out the significance of listening. He suggests that group sessions begin as unstructured as possible, perhaps with just a simple opening statement or comment. He suggests that the utterances, whether significant or superficial, are worth listening to in a group setting. Rogers also refers to Reik's "Third Ear" concept as a valuable listening tool as an approach to enhancing growth in the group process. Rogers points out a position, with which I agree, that the counselor can re-experience the experiences of the client empathetically by understanding the motivations of human behavior." One might safely conclude that what is not said verbally by the hurting person is in a number of situations more important to determining needs than what is said verbally. Listening is the deliberate effort or ability; based upon training insights and a willingness, to hear what is being said in the disguise of a number of statements. Listening is a prerequisite to healing. Should one avoid the opportunity of listening, hearing will not be realized.

William Glasser in his book, Stations of the Mind, talks about "The **Perceptual** Systems" which lie suggests involves three basic perceptions: controlled, uncontrolled and a new-information perception. He suggests ten orders through which it is possible for information to travel. He feels that most new information passes through the controlled perception and the uncontrolled perception orders, but that they may enter at any order. He seems to say that the ideal order of entry is the sixth order because at the sixth order there tends to be less fragmentation and that a much clearer perception takes place.' What this says to me is that perceptions are based upon individual backgrounds and experience, and that there needs to be adequate time given for reflection upon and the processing of data before needs are effectively met. Thus, reflection and processing are closely akin to, if not, the core of listening with the result being hearing.

Literally, I was born with a third ear. It was literally located beneath the ear on the right side of my head. While the evolutionary process literally wore it away and only a small sign of it remains, I sometimes raise the question of myself in the light of my lack of listening skills if I have lost my figurative, technical third ear. This is an area in which I have concentrated a significant amount of effort and energy during The United States Army Command and General Staff College Course (CRCGSC) Phases 1, 11, 111.

While the monster has not been totally conquered and destroyed, I know more about his location in "Lock Nest" and some of the tools I need to actualize his gradual capture and destruction. I would like to claim the power of hearing him scream and then being able to distinguish between his actual cries for help and those cries that are false and unrelated.

1. BIBLICAL BASES FOR ACTIVE LISTENING

While the Holy Bible was not originally intended to be a blanket answer-book to all of the problems, questions, and situations of all time and history, it seems to me that there are a lot of wholesome insights and answers offered that are applicable to contemporary problems, questions and situations. Sociologists and psychiatrists have put us in touch with certain psychosomatic phenomena and the makeup of human personality. But there are aspects of wan (genetically used) of which the Bible gives clearer understandings and treatments: sin, evil, fallen nature and salvation.

Paul Tillich, the philosopher-theologian, who performed a marriage between the two sciences with his method of Correlation, has also raised an ontological question, the answers to which are dependent upon the findings of a finite jury. Tillich raise the question: "What is being itself?" The question moves one from the epistemological to the ontological, or from how we get knowledge to what knowledge is. Tillich suggest that being is that which always is. It is not simply the ground of being, it is being itself. The point here is not to enter into a philosophical and theological dissertation; instead, it is to suggest that the root of, or the basis of all human hurt is possibly sin. Sin here is to mean disobedience to God and to the natural laws.

This is a rather limited and/or abridged treatment of what I consider to be a universal human predicament; but the focus here is not specifically hamartiology, but generally, theology. As the Bible offers bases for the understanding and treatment of a large number of human problems, I feel very strongly that I can turn to the Bible for insights as to enhancing and utilizing listening skills.

A. The Old Testament

Both Old and New Testament scholarship has referred to the Bible as "The Book of Books", or a library of sixty-six books between two covers. The etymology of the world bible, "biblos" which got its name from the papyri plant of the Nile River, originally meant book. For Pastoral Care, from a biblical perspective, the Bible is the book that serves as a basic source and norm upon which the Christian care-givers authority is based. The bulk of the remainder of this paper shall focus upon those biblical bases upon which I feel Pastoral Care stands and a theological treatment of those texts that might enhance the care-giver's skills.

Paul Tillich, Rudolph Bultman and R.C. Briggs emphasize tile significance of symbolism in theological language. Tillich says, in essence, that theology is culturalogical in the sense that theological relevance is expressed in the comprehensible thoughts and symbols of the audience to which it seeks to serve. Bultman says that theology is basically mythological in the sense that it is human language that attempts to talk about a phenomenon, or phenomena, that transcends the human. Therefore, whatever we say about the beyond-the-human in human language is an approximation and can never capture the total essence of that about which we speak. Robert C. Briggs suggest that the historical-critical Methodology (Form, Source, Textual and Redaction criticism) is a most valuable hermeneutical tool that helps us to dispel the myths associated with the New Testament.

The bulk of biblical writings are veiled in symbolic and allegorical language. Therefore, to understand the meaning of the message, one needs to get behind the symbols that stand before the message. That seems to me to have a direct correlation to active listening, non-verbal and body language. Notorious for that style of writings is apocalyptic literature in both Old and New Testaments: Daniel Ezekiel, Mark, Matthew and the book of Revelation, to mention only a few. Much of what is communicated to those of us in the care-giving profession is through coded and mixed symbols and signs. Therefore, it seems quite significant to me that an understanding of the signs and symbols of those whom we seek to help is an indispensable prerequisite to offering help.

The point of departure to the exploration examination of biblical texts and passages that reflect an acute listen and a perspicuous hearing seems logically to be Genesis, the book of beginnings. Immediately following the creation of man in the "I" account (Genesis 2:18-23) God senses a need of man, Adam. "It is not good for man to be alone" is one textual treatment of the "J" account while others vary from "it is not right" "It is not fair" for man to be alone. The point here is not to enter into Textual criticism, rather it is to focus on the divine acts of listening and hearing.

I doubt very seriously that Adam or Adamah (mankind) verbalized to God that you have treated me unfairly at the point of creation. But the fact of God's recognition by Adam's affect a degree of incompleteness suggest to me that God is quite adequate in sensing body language.

Anthropomorphism is a word used sometimes in theological circles to talk about, or ascribe human-like qualities to superhuman or to divine beings. To say that God hears is to assign Him ears, but human language is so finite and limited that through it we are never able to fully understand all there is about God. Thus, an approximation is to ascribe to Him the sense of hearing, tasting, feeling, etcetera. The Bible is filled with a wide variety of situations in which God is suggested to have listened The most significant passage in the Old Testament agreed to by a number of black theologians whose focus is on liberation, is Exodus 3:7-8: "... I have surely seen the affliction of my people...and have heard their cry...and I am come down to deliver them..." In these two verses the writer of the text, Moses, ascribes to God the sense of seeing and hearing. It is interesting that immediately following seeing comes hearing, and based upon the two, God says "... I know their sorrows." What seems quite significant here for Pastoral Care-givers is that based upon certain perceived facts following seeing and hearing, God arrived at certain conclusions as to the needs of a people and that the identifying of the needs proceeded delivery. It is inconceivable as to the ultimate outcome of Israelite history had God not listened to the cries and needs of a people expressed in non-verbal, symbols and gestures.

The Exodus account, historically, is the single most important event in the life of the people of Israel the world over. It is the point at which they became a nation and it serves as the paradigm, archetype upon which their whole life is ordered.

It is the point in their historical, cultural and religious experiences where God, the care-giver, remained silent long enough to move beyond what the tongue and mouth said and heard the internal and affective groans of a people. The people of Israel sought to transmit such a significant event to unborn generations to come. God's response to a people's cry and the corresponding delivery to people-hood and their nationhood suggests a God who gets involved in the existential concerns and affairs of peoples.

As has been suggested and pointed out above, the Hebrews ascribed human-like characteristics to God. Theologically, this is known as anthropomorphism. While this God to whom they referred and sought to tangibilitate and relativize was transcendent they sought to make and understand Him as being immanent within His creation and, to know that He was quite involved in the affairs of his creatures. The human attempt and effort to actualize that conceptualization of God was to express it in the most available medium, human language. Human language that seeks to talk about or to capture the essence of God is mythological; at best, it is a mere approximation because it is humans 'attempt to express in human terms that which is not fully human. Therefore, to suggest that God heard implies that there was a time or, that there are times when God does not hear. To suggest that God did not hear at one point implies a limited God, which is counter to the concept of El Shaddai, God Almighty. I feel very strongly that while God is omnipotent, He does choose to limit himself at times. One would raise the question as to the whereabouts of God during Auschwitz, or during more than three-hundred years of black slavery in the United States and the earthquake in Bangladesh? or the tsunomia, or the disease, the hunger and poverty in Africa. The easy answer is to say I do not know! A mother answer is. God chose to limit Himself during these moments in human history.

But, then surfaces the why question: why and for what reason did God choose to be silent or have his hearing-impaired during one situation and hears so well and become actively involved in other situations? It seems appropriate at this juncture to ascribe to God the qualities of active and passive listening.

There are a number of black theologians and sociologists who have alluded to God as a white racist and slave master in the sense that they have seen Him taking the side of the whites against the blacks during such a long period of American history. For me, that is too radical an approach and it loses its theological significance for me and degenerates itself to inappropriately expressed anger. What is significant for me is to ascribe to God the qualities of passive and active listening. This suggests to me that God always hears in either one of the two human understandings of hearing. Suffice it to say that within the context of this paper, adequate time and attention have been accorded the manner in which God listens. Therefore, the bulk of the remainder of this paper will focus upon biblical passages, which reflect listening on the part of God, the corresponding theological significance, and its implications for the delivery of Pastoral Care.

It has been my understanding that passivity implies the opposite of activity. It implies non-involvement, distance, detachment and remoteness. Passivity creates a barrier between objects and between people impedes effectiveness in relationships, be they pastoral or social. The God of the Bible is portrayed as a God of involvement who came to where people were somehow conditions, situations and people were no longer the same, following a visit from God. In her book, Words Made Flesh, Frank Ferder points out in Chapter Two, "On that day God listened", the role and significance of listening as a biblical stance toward creation. She seems to suggest that there is more to contemplation than simply sitting out on a log with your head in your lap or looking skyward, but an actual time of silence where hearing is possible. Abraham Heschel in his book The Sabbath, points out Hebraic significance of the creation story's usage of the word "rested." The Hebrew word is menuha, which means "purposeful contemplation." Herschel defines menuha as a process through which "...one becomes quiet enough inside to see more deeply into life." This suggest to me the role of silence in hearing. It is an act at a time in one's life or during one's efforts to be pastoral that the care- ceases to verbalize and listens to both the verbal and the non-verbal of the patient and gathers from what transpires or what fails to transpire the needs of the patient, and perhaps his own needs.

While the primary role of the care-giver is not to meet his own personal needs, menuha (silence) will also allow one to become aware of self-needs.

The word hearing is used in the Bible to mean different functions at different times in history and in a person's life. In the book of Job, which is believed to be one of the oldest books of the Old Testament, 4:16, there are employed several interesting terms: "... stood still and silence." After standing still the author mentioned that he heard. The point is that stood still and silence preceded hearing. The quote in question is one, which involves Job and God where Job listens to God and, as a result, hears what it is that God says. The book of Job, a part of the Wisdom Literature of the Old Testament, emphasizes active listening and the opposite of such is vividly illustrated in the visits of Job's three friends, if you might call them such. Job's friends sought to answer Job's questions based upon their prior historical agenda. While they did sit quietly for several days, they were unable to listen beyond the scopes of their own religious traditions to another level of needs. They sought to answer Job out of their traditional seminary exposures, cultural biases, and their one-perspective inclinations without ever listening to and hearing another perspective of equal validity. My own early attempts at Pastoral Care reflect a close similarity to that offered by Job's friends. I was agenda-oriented, time conscious and had a need to get my point across. I was unusually uncomfortable with silence and I am certain that I missed a lot of opportunities for a much more effective ministry by just saying word to keep things moving. The tremendous amount of time, energy and effort 1 have put *into* enhancing my listening and hearing skills have enabled me to realize significant growth as a care-giver in 2005.

The idea of contemplation, or menuha and hovering, coupled with motion or activity seem to me to be an applicable description of the creative process. God hovers over His world and notices chaos, disorder and incompleteness. He creates in six days' order out of chaos, and after the creative process is complete, on the seventh day, He rests, contemplates, listens and hears. The number seven in Hebrew thought implies completion, wholeness, universality and perfection. There seems to be implied in these concepts a God who actively listens or, at least, who is capable of listening and hearing. Thus, out of this concept, emerges the understanding that God is actively listening, contemplating, making whole and bringing about perfection in an imperfect cosmos. Thus, the exhortation of Saint Paul: "...all things are working together for good to their that love God..." (Romans 8:28), seems to suggest that God is at work on my behalf by hearing my groans.

The noun hearing and the corresponding verb hear are utilized in both the Old and New Testaments to refer to both human and spiritual, or religious activities. There are times when hear means to respond to what God has said, as is seen in Deuteronomy 31: 12-13, which suggests that one proves that he has heard God if he fears Him. The writer of the Deuteronomy passage is emphasizing the importance of fearing or respecting and reverencing God, but that fear emerges as a result of really hearing or understanding what it is that God has said. The textual references on the subject of hearing are too numerous to do an exhaustive or justifiable treatment of each of them within the context of this little book, therefore selected scriptures will be examined from Old and New Testament texts.

Job's expressed desire in 31:35 sounds like a universal cry made by peoples of all ages, all periods of history, and of all cultural perspectives. While Job's expressions come out of the despair of the hour and were directed to a universal rather than a specific audience or group of persons, it is safe to say, based upon the context of Jobs situation, that he was dismissing his so-called friends or Pastoral Care-givers. For while they sit and look at him with contempt and sarcasm, they are not hearing what Job says. Therefore, he sorts of dismisses them: "Oh that one would hear me." Job sounds like patient X on Ward Universal who is now experiencing visit number three by Pastoral Care-giver Doe. Doe has been doing a lot of verbal work and offering a lot of advice, but there has been very little or no listening occurring. The patient has spoken to the counselor verbally and affectively, but Doe has not heard him. He has spoken through gestures and eye contact, but after three visits of thirty in invites each, he has not been heard. The patient gathers from what is taking place and from what is not taking place that his counselor has a fixed agendum and that what he is feeling and thinking is of secondary significance. It is at that point that the patient X", Job cries out: "Oh that one would hear me!" for a change!

Job's dilemma or the counselor's dilemma is not necessarily foreign to our experiences today. As I have pointed out above, I too have failed to hear what parishioners and patients have said to me because of my lack of listening skills. While examining, over a period of time, and critiquing Pastoral Care Reports (PCR's) complied by a number of Clinical Pastoral Care (CPE) students, and in reviewing my own behavior during counseling sessions, I leave noticed a number of points at which valuable insights into the real concerns of the patients were overlooked simply because the students did not listen.

In one or two reports, the student enters the rooms and goes into the "standard ritual" of Good afternoon, I'm

Chaplain Doe, how are you today?" to which the reply comes, "Oh, just fine Chaplain!"; the students pick up on the "Just fine" and not on the inconsistency between hospitalization and just fine. The question here is if he is just fine, for what reason is he here? If the student had really listened to the body language of the patient he would have heard, perhaps, an attempt to cover up, minimize or even deny the seriousness of the patient's medical or mental condition.

As has been noted briefly above, the verb in the Bible has a number of meanings depending upon the context in which it is used for the times to which it speaks. The meaning of the verb hear in Hebrew poetry and wisdom literature is to adhere to the logic and wisdom by acting them out in one's conduct and behavior. Both in Proverbs 22:17 and Ecclesiastes 5:1 are strong suggestions that to hear is to apply. The implications are that if one does not put into practice, he has not heard. Isaiah 6:9 is a reference to the physiological organ, the ear, where the Prophet suggests that the people hear but do not understand; they see, but are unable to perceive the content and the relevancy for their lives. Isaiah 55:3 is an exhortation to adhere to, with the results being life.

The ancient Israelites were keenly aware of nature and they were also attuned to natural phenomena. The earth and the world in which they lived taught them to listen to nature and to be wise. But, in addition to their need to be good listeners, they understood themselves as being created in the image of God and thus able to look beyond the observable, hear beyond what was verbalized and grasp the grit-level meanings of that which was being communicated. In the simple usage of the term hearing, it was getting beneath the surface of their lives to the real issues of life.

The exhortation of Isaiah in 50:4-5, "The Lord Yahweh has opened my ear", is not an acknowledgment or celebration of an instantaneous opening of the physiological ear, rather it is a celebration or an acknowledgment that I have just really heard the Lord. For Isaiah, responding is a result of listening and listening seems to be an ability provided by God. God and man are partners in the healing process, to deny one at the expense of the others is to deny a significant reality in Pastoral Care. The Holy Spirit surrounds us, overshadows us, invades us and enables us to hear that which is not necessarily articulated verbally.

Adequate attention has been given to the biblical bases for active listening in the delivery of Pastoral Care. The focus will now shift to actual biblical situations in which active listening became the indispensable key that opened the door and provided insights into the below-the-surface problems and made possible the delivery of Pastoral Care.

The Old Testament Prophets and Seers, were accorded an unusual amount of accolades and were awarded numerous honorific titles for the quality insights and for the quality of prophetic messages they delivered to the nation. While I do not wish to negate, minimize or discredit the abilities of the great men of Israel, I am toying with the possibility and probability that much of what the Prophets saw and pointed out was based not upon divine intervention, but rather upon the abilities of the prophets to listen to nature, history, and to verbal and now-verbal affects. The Prophets and Seers were children of their day, aware of their history, and were very much in touch with the psychology of human personality. The prophets were able to observe the current behaviors of men and nations, reflect back upon their history and arrive at a conclusion which suggested that if your behavior does not change, your future is obvious.

The Prophets and Seers of the Old Testament cannot be denied the ability to read the language of people and of nations; therefore, the rebuke, "...these people worship me with their lips, but their hearts are far from me." The obvious was the in congruencies between what was being said and what was done. The care giver who is keenly aware of these incongruences and inconsistencies will detect them and look beyond the presenting surface data to the real issues and concerns of the patient. It is that ability to stop, look and listen before proceeding to just do something, that enhances the quality of Pastoral ministry.

The biblical writers had at their disposal voluminous materials and experiences upon which they could draw in compiling books, letters, and oracles. However, they were very eclectic, selective and analytical in their approach to writing. There was much more to be said of Cyrus of Persia than was said in the biblical record but, for some reason, the authors chose not to leave us a total treatment of his life and works. The same principle is to be adhered to here, in that selective passages and events are to be treated so as to focus upon the basic theme of the paper.

B. The New Testament

The Fourth Gospel has been described by a number of New Testament scholars as the book signs. The signs suggest that john selects from a wide-range of works in the life of the historical Jesus and chooses seven of them, and with the seven works or miracles he captures the total essence of the work of Christ.

In that sense, the Fourth Gospel is more Christological than it is historical or chronological. The primary motive in John, as is true of the Synoptic Gospel, is to show the person and works of Jesus Christ, the Pre-existent Logos. The seven signs of John commence with the wedding at Cana of Galilee where he turns water into wine and concludes with the chief sign, the raising of Lazarus from the dead, or the resuscitation of Lazarus. Both the Synoptic and John used a number of the same stories, but the Synoptic used a great deal more of them than did John in his writing of the Fourth Gospel. In the Fourth Gospel, 4:46-54, is an incident in which Jesus immediately focuses on the affect and raises a concern that forces the official to be specific "...he went unto him, and besought him that he would come down, and heal his son..." Jesus replied to the request "Except ye see signs and wonders, ye will not believe." The question comes to mind as to why Jesus would reply to the official in such a manner and with such words? I gather from Jesus' reply that after Jesus read his affect, his history and the cultural expectations of the official, he immediately became aware of a beneath-the-surface request to come to the house of the great one, perform some signs before the crowds, meal his son and my personal status will be enhanced. Jesus was able to pick rip on the double message, pointed them out to the man and introduced the man to an effective approach to healing minus the signs and fanfare. Jesus' ability to listen to and hear what was said verbally and non-verbally in this visit was both confrontative and facilitative: it forced the man to clear up his priorities and focus on the crisis. The request shifted from "... come heal my son to if you do not come my son will die or is dead." It seems rather strange that a man of status, power, and influence, whose life revolved around giving orders, would, ask Jesus to do less. Notice he did not ask Jesus to simply give the order, he asked him to come personally. The underlying or ulterior motive, I suspect was to use the weak and dying condition of his son to get himself catapulted into history. For to have him who only a few days ago had changed water into wine come to his house, would have been of further indication of his greatness and make the work of Jesus of secondary importance.

At this point I am forced as a" sometimes theologian" and professional caregiver to raise a rhetorical question which will hardly go unnoticed by those who are critical and confrontative: What does the incident cited above have to do with Pastoral Care? The question is an excellent one even if I did raise it myself. The delivery of a commodity that is pre-packaged and one that may be delivered on-demand or on request is as my daughter would say: "Dad that sounds cold." I take her to mean by coldness, a remoteness, a distance, a lack of involvement, or out of touch, and a lack of compassion. For the care-giver to pre-package his goods prior to departing the office to visit a patient and merely deliver it is rather cold in the sense of the definition offered above. This are not to suggest that the care-giver does not have skills, tools and approaches to ministry, but rather it is to suggest that one uses those professional assets to ascertain the patient's agenda, clarify concerns, check out behavior, confront, and based upon the data gained one proceeds to offer Pastoral Care. The meaning of the incident above lies in the fact that Jesus used his Pastoral skills and insights to help the man to get in touch with what was more important, his son's imminent death and not fanfare and popularity in the front yard of his house.

It has been said that the difference between Pastoral Care and Pastoral Counseling is that in the former the pastor goes to the patient and in the latter, the patient seeks out the pastor. With that d differentiation in mind, the story of the miraculous draught of fishes on the Lake of Gennesaret is a perfect example of Pastoral Care in the sense that Jesus sent to them and sought them out. Theologically, most of the Lukan narratives are preoccupied with the underdog: the poor, the weak, the disinherited, women, and the outcast. While in a sense the fisherman whose barren and unfruitful night on the lake might reflect a number of the theological foci of Luke, the significance for me here is Jesus' amazing ability to focus on that which was primary and foremost. The twenty-first-century mind can hardly imagine the degree of trauma produced by the first-century mentality by a barren and fruitless night on the lake; the least we might gather from the incident is its morale-demeaning effect, the negative reflection upon their reputation as fishermen and the threat to their livelihood as commercial fishermen. There is the sense of defeat, failure and loss; there is the question of status, image and future that must be passing through the mind of Peter, yet he never feels comfortable mentioning what must be a part of the subconscious to Jesus. Had it not been for the keen insights of the Pastoral Care-giver who came to Peter in his lowest moments, looked beyond the external behavior of washing nets like a successful fisherman, challenged him to face reality and to participate in altering his situation, history would still read, no fish today! It is not known exactly how Jesus picked up on Peter's affect and sensed a bit of disgust; I would suggest however, that Jesus listened more to what Peter did not say verbally than to the verbal expressions. It is particularly true here that what a person does not say is sometimes more significant than what he says. This miracle, or the pastoral care done in this story, suggest a keen sense of listening, which made possible effective Pastoral Care.

The phenomenal insights of Jesus are demonstrated further in Mark 1:22-28 where a demoniac came to Jesus in the Synagogue and accorded him the honorific title "Holy one of God" which Jesus could have accepted at face value. Jesus knew that he was the Holy one of God and he did not deny that, but what he read was the ulterior motive of the person who made the claim. Was it an attempt on the part of the demon-possessed to shift the attention of Jesus from ridding people of demoniac spirits and focus the attention on Jesus himself? I have a sneaking suspicion that a close parallel exits between this event and the temptation event where the devil seeks to have Jesus refocus his attention on the temporary and impermanent, rather than on the eternal and permanent.

It seems safe for me to assume that the primary focus of the New Testament writers was not Clinical Pastoral Education per se, nevertheless, I feel very strongly that I have the theological license to explore, analyze, interpret and to make relevant applications of the words of the text to the contemporary setting. It seems perfectly legitimate to rue to deduce front the stories and pericopia of the Bible certain meanings for today. For the Bible not only speaks to men and women of the remote and distant past, it speaks to us today. Were the former only true, then the Bible might have outlived its useful ness and thus become a dead book.

There is a song in the black religious experience that say he looks beyond our faults and sees our needs. The song was not written by a mainline theologian nor a CPE supervisor, or a CPE student for that matter, but the message is skill-enhancing for me as a care-giver. The song suggests to me that God in Christ sometimes looks beyond where I am, to where I really am in the sense of need. The passage in Luke 7:11-17 is a vivid example of a Christ who looked beyond the obvious to the submerged arid unarticulated. Let us look at the quote: "Not when he came high to the gate of the city. Behold, there was a dead man carried out, the only son of his mother, and she was a widow: and much people of the city was with her ...and when the Lord saw her" (not the son) "He had compassion on her" (not the son).

The results of the encounter are a part of the biblical record, but what is quite significant for me is Jesus' keen ability to pick up on the real issues of the hour. The issue, or the concern, was not that her son was dead, the concern was that it was her only son and that she was a widow. For what reason would the loss of an only son and her being a widow in pact upon the need of the hour, is the question.

Luke does not take us on a CPE journey at this point, nevertheless, I am forced by the nature of this book to raise the question: 'as the mother's tears based primarily upon a death'* or upon the sudden loss of financial support? The words of Luke, "her only son and she was a widow" raise some concerns for me. The concerns stem from the close similarity that exists between the Elijah and Elisha incidents in the Old Testament: both of whom restored to life a young boy, and an only son (I Kings 17:17-24, II Kings 4:18-37).

In the Elijah story, the mother is a widow as is true in the Lukan narrative. Based upon Luke's theology, which is heavily focused on women, the poor, and the weak, I would strongly suggest that Luke's attempt here is to point out Jesus' identity with the disinherited of society. This seems to me to be a Lukan theological motif.

The relevancy of the acts of Jesus in this Lukan narrative for the care-giver is the fact that he read more than the obvious: a dead person. For Luke he was not just a dead boy, he represented the hopes, dreams, livelihood and future of a poor widow. It seems deliberate, given Luke's approach to theology, for Luke to use the material of the oral tradition to dramatize Jesus' Christology. I am not sure as to Luke's source, M or Q, for the material, nor why the story is unique for him in the Synoptic; it seems safe to say that he had a specific motive, which is suggested above by the present writer. Luke carefully selects his words as if he has just completed supervisory CPE at a famous CPE center. Listen to his diction: the boy was dead, as opposed to demised, passed, or asleep. He is specific as to the family make up: an only son of a widow. With this data available to the Pastoral Care-giver, ministry can now take a sharper, a more direct and a more specific focus. This biblical selection further emphasizes the significance of active listening in the delivery of Pastoral Care.

In examining the biblical texts in search of theological bases for active listening in the delivery of Pastoral Care, one finds a large number of selections that hold great possibilities for Pastoral Care and the significance of active listening. The New Testament writers never cease to amaze me at their usage of language. In Matthew 9:2 is the term: "When Jesus saw their faith." The ink mediate question is how is it possible to see faith? Obviously, the theologian has a specific purpose in mind. While we are unable to get into the mind of the writer, we can look at him through the eyes of theologians. Obviously faith, as an abstract and an intangible concept, was not literally seen by Jesus. Therefore, it seems to me that the writer is suggesting that Jesus looked beyond the crowds that brought the paralyzed boy to him and saw the act as an external, visible result of an internal faith in Christ. Without asking a lot of questions, Jesus immediately pronounced the man's sins forgiven.

There is very little question, based on the text, that those who brought the boy to Jesus had an extremely deep faith in Jesus; but there is a significant and abrupt change in the event. It is obvious that the boy was in need of physical healing, but Jesus never mentions the physical condition rather he forgave his sins. This does not suggest to me that his physical condition was unimportant, instead, it seems to be part of the theologian's attempt to point out a direct connection between the boy's physical condition and sin. The present writer does not agree that sin's results are necessarily revealed in physical deformity or sickness. Obviously, this is the understanding of the writer of the book of Matthew. The writer seems to suggest that Jesus, while concerned about the physical need, saw a much deeper spiritual need, therefore taking care of the more serious need first, eventually took care of the less serious need secondly.

The Old and New Testaments are filled with events, stories and incidents in which both spiritual and physical healing occurred. What is most significant, it seems to me, is that the care-givers were active listeners and that active listening enabled them to identify issues and concerns that were not necessarily verbalized by the hurting persons. Based upon the theological, historical and biblical evidence pointed out in this book, it seems to me that in addition to the large number of technical tools available to us as care- givers, the Bible has unlimited bases for active listening in the delivery of pastoral care.

---

[11] Carl Rogers on Encounters Group (New York: Harper & Row, 1970), p. 47.

[12] William Glasser, Stations of the Mind. (Philadelphia: Harper & Row, 1981), pp. 99-105.

[13] Paul Tillich. Systematic Theology, Vol. I. (Chicago: The University of Chicago Press, 1951), pp. 163-174.

[14] John H. Hayes. Introduction to the Bible. (Philadelphia: The Westminster Press, 1976), pp. 5-8.

[15] James Cone. A Black Theology of Liberation. (New York: J. B. Lippencott Company, 1970), pp. 212-220.

[16] Fran Ferder Word Made Flesh. (Notre Dame: Ave Maria Press, 1986), pp. 3-35.

[17] Walter T. Eichrodt. Theology of the Old Testament, Vol. II, Trans. by: J. A. Baker, (Philadelphia: The

Westminster Press, 1967), pp. 134-142.

18 Abraham Heschel. <u>The Sabbath.</u> (New York: Farrar, Straus & Girous, 1978). pp. 22-24.

19 Walter Eichrodt. Theology of the Old testament. Vol II. Trans. by: J.A Baker (Philadelphia: The Westminster Press, 1967), p. 73.

CONCLUSIONS

The thesis of this book is that there are sufficient biblical bases to support the active listening approach to the delivery of Pastoral Care. Because the pastor is primarily a theologian, an attempt was made to reflect upon and reacquaint ourselves with the theological process, its historical and existential functions, and the theological licenses available to us to use the word of God in our ministry. To suggest that this paper has exhausted all of the possibilities and tapped all of the resources available to us would not only be presumptuous, but it would also be bordering on idolatry. Nevertheless, at the risk of being charged with both, I have been so audacious as to attempt to explore an area that seems to hold some insights for me in my effort to help the hurting. I trust that the critical reader will find a bit of identity with me in this struggle and offer additional insights that were not a part of my own insights.

Theological insights into new and more effective approaches to ministry is the primary focus of this book. The idea of exploring more positive biblical bases for what I do and am about as a minister of the Word and Sacrament was born some years ago during my struggles in CPE, and I have taken the time to reflect and finally articulate on paper my feelings and growth. While I was somewhat aware of the significance of active listening as a more effective approach listening as informed through secular and academic disciplines, I felt a need to explore the Bible for additional skill-enhancing approaches to Pastoral Care. Amazingly enough, my exploration of the Bible revealed a number of bases to support the thesis, and the hypotheses I hold of the Bible and related materials hold great insights and bases to support the significance of active listening in the delivery of Pastoral Care. As is true of all quality research, its findings are tentative rather than conclusive.

APPENDIX A

A. Pastoral Care Report (Mrs. J)

The Minister

Name Of Patient: Mrs. J

Date of visit:

Religion: Protestant

Number of Visits: One Sex: Female
(Pre-op)

Length of visit: 10 minutes Age: 54

Date of presentation: Military   Status:
Dependent Retired Wife
Army Officer

1. NARRATIVE

While doing my pre-ops on 10 January at approximately 1430 hours, I visited the room of the above mentioned patient. She was a very cordial person who when she saw me enter the room said, "Hi! Chaplain. I inquired as to which of them was Mrs. J and she quickly identified herself as Mrs. J, My initial reaction was amazement because I did not expect such a salutation from a lady who was involved in a conversation with three other roommates. After I quickly recomposed myself, I replied: "Hello, I'm Chaplain Doe. The verbatim narrative will reflect the brief exchange, which followed. The room was well - lighted and quite tidy. There were flowers, cards and other expressions of love and concern. I present this PCR because of the anger I perceived she had. I am aware that a number of mu PCR's have reflected my perception of anger in patients and my concerns is: am I seeing in others what might be my own anger? I am not in touch with that anger but I solicit the group's perceptions of Chaplain Doe in terms of the anger he/I might have.

VERBATIM

c1 All, hello, I'm Chaplain Doe

p1 Hello, Chaplain, come on in. How are you tonight?

c2 Just fine. How are you?

p2 Oh, just fine Chaplain (she has a face full of smiles caught me by surprise. I expected a patient-facing surgery to have a little worry on her face but she was lit up with smiles).

c3 I'm the duty chaplain. I noticed that you are scheduled for surgery tomorrow, and I came by to visit with you prior to your surgery.

p3 That is good Chaplain. It is good to see you. (with so many smiles and good-to-see-you's I sensed that she wanted more than she 2 or 3 minutes of my time).

c4 How do you feel about surgery on tomorrow?

p4 Great. It is time now. My husband has had his share and now it is my time.

c5 Your time

p5 Yes Chaplain. My husband has had (she mentioned every disease in the book), all of these and then surgery. He has been through so much. I just feel so sorry for hint. He has gotten more than his share.

c6 Huh!

p6 But he strong. He can take it so well. I told him do not get sick, let me go, it is my time wow. (She is still full of smiles). So I will be wheeled in there in the morning and get it over.

c7 Sounds like a lot is happening.

p7 Yes it is Chaplain, but I'm going to hang in there. It is my time now

c8 Uh! What does your time mean?

p8 Well my husband has been through so much sickness. (She pauses, looks at the floor and ceiling, and then she focuses on me) Chaplain, it is not fair.

c9 Oh! (I just stand there and look at her)

p9 It is not fair for my husband to have to go through so much.

c10 Huh!

p10 Yes, so much and I not have some too.

c11 How do you feel about what is happening to you?

p11 What's happening to me is nothing compared to my husband.

c12 Sound concerned about your husband?

p12 Yes Chaplain. It is not fair for all that to happen to one person. He is such a good man.

c13 It is not fair for all this to happen to you?

p13 (This questions seemed to have caught her by surprise. She had to take a few moments to reflect) I guess not, Chaplain. No, it is not fair. There are a lot of people not half as good as me and my husband and this will never happen to them.

c14 Or to you?

p14 Yes Chaplain. I found a lump in my breast (she points to her left breast) just in time they say. So I will be able to get it all taken care of and go back home.

c16 Mrs. J, how do you feel about surgery on tomorrow?

p16 (She pauses for a while) chaplain, I'm a little concerned. If said I was not, I would not, be telling the truth.

c17 Mrs. J, you have mentioned a lot of things to me.

p17 Thank you Chaplain. I really do need you and your prayers. (She would not let go of my hands. I was getting concerned as to what the 3 other ladies in the room were thinking. She finally let go).

c18 Let us pray. (We join hands again) God our Father, I pray your blessings upon this woman. May you be with her tonight and during surgery on tomorrow. I pray her husband. Might you give him the strength he needs for now and for days ahead. Let them know that you love and care for them regardless of what happens in their lives. In Christ's name I pray. Amen.

p18 (She opens her eyes while still holding my hand tightly and says): Thank you Chaplain. If you get a chance come back again.

c19 You are quite welcome. I will plan to do that if you are here long enough.

p19 Goodbye, Chaplain.

EVALUATION: To be honest, I do not really know where this woman was. She initially came across as being quite happy which looked and seemed a little abnormal for a person facing what she was on tomorrow, so I tried to get into that. I'm not sure I did. My feeling was that she felt hurt, anger and fear. I also got the feeling that she had a need to be a strong woman for her husband and the chaplain. She was another person who needed to come across a "Peter, the Big Fisherman", but knew that what she faced on tomorrow was too much for her to face alone. The assurance I gave her of both my presence with her and God's, seemed to be what she needed most. While I had to struggle to stay with her, her struggle was greater than mine.

THEOLOGICAL REFLECTIONS: Theologically the woman is a reflection of hypocritical religiosity. She comes across initially as a strong person who has not a worry in the world and later almost crumbled at the idea of her husband 'having enough" which might have meant that she has had enough and chose to project the issue on her husband. I also got the feeling that she had a need to be strong for her husband and would not dare let him see her cry. The constant reference that it is her time now might indicate that she felt that she was the person who needed the punishment for some misdeed she had committed and had escaped his eye or knowledge. She seemed to have wanted to say I'm guilty but I did not pry deeply enough to ever know if that was the case. I am not able to recollect a biblical passage that is reflective of the woman's presenting condition.

APPENDIX B

B. Pastoral Care Report (Mrs. S, 7 Dec 85)

Rev. J. Doe   Name of Patient: Mrs. S

Date of Visit: 7 Dec 85   Religion: Protestant

Number of Visits: One   Sex: Female

Length of visit: ¾ Hour   Age: 58

Date of presentation 4 Feb Ward: 67
86

Military Status: Dependent Wife of Retired Army MSG

NARRATIVE

Upon my arrival on Ward 67, I immediately consulted the patient cards to determine the religious preference of each patient in my area of responsibility. I had no unusual reason of visiting her; she was one of the patients whose card indicated the protestant preference. I entered the room and introduced myself as the ward chaplain – That I had stopped by to visit with her. The room was a 4-bed room and she was one of two people currently occupying the room. There were very few cards (2 or 3), no flowers or other symbols of love, care or concern. The curtains were open and quite a bit of light was entering through the window. She seemed to be in deep thought–sort of detached from her immediate world and her surroundings. I am presenting this PCR as a way of letting the group see what I did. This is an attempt to get feedback from the group as to how I might have been more facilitative in her dealing with her immediate and future condition. I ask the group to take special note of that I have done better theologically and pastorally.

VERBATIM

c1 Good afternoon, I'm Chaplain Doe.

p1 Good afternoon, Chaplain, how are you?

c2 I'm fine, how are today?

p2 Well, Ok, I guess.

c3 You don't sound too sure?

p3 They have me scheduled for surgery and I have never had surgery before. (Pause, head down, then she looks up at me.

c4 Sounds like you have some concerns about the surgery?

p4 Yes Chaplain, I do. This has really been a testing time for me. I have never had this happen to me before. Doctors!!!

c5 It is probably normal for people who are facing surgery to have some concerns. But you also mentioned "testing time". What do you mean by that?

p5 I'm the pastor of my church back home and I have always had faith in God to heal me so I have not been to the doctors.

c6 You've had faith that God would heal you and he has not so you had to come to the hospital?

p6 Will he heal me Chaplain?

c7 Do you feel that he can heal you here in the hospital?

p7   Yes I do. I have faith in my God and whenever He gets ready, He will heal me.

c8   I can really appreciate your faith in God to heal you and I would support you in your faith, but you mentioned "doctors" and that you are the pastor of your church. How do feel about doctors?

p8   Well, they are Ok, but God is the healer.

c9   Yes God is the healer. But how does that make you feel about doctors?

p9   I do not want them to cut on me.

c10 Yes, I think I can understand that, but you seem to be turned off at doctors?

p10 In my church, Chaplain, we believe in divine healing. We do not go to the doctors.

c11 What, does divine healing mean to you?

p11 Well, God is my healer. We wait on Him to heal us.

c12 Tiy said, "We wait on Him to heal us", Who are we and us?

p12 The members of my church.

c13 How long does it take for God to heal you?

p13 His own time.

c14 Could that be a week, two months, a year, or a lifetime?

p14 Different times. Sometimes it's longer than other times.

c15 How long has it been for you?

p15 Well, about 5 years.

c16 If God does not heal you, what would you think of Him?

p16 He never fails, He never fails.

c17 It has been five years now for you, suppose it takes another five or longer?

p17 I don't think it will take that long.

c18 Do you feel that perhaps the doctors here can help your healing?

p18 They seem to think so.

c19 What do you think.

p19 I just do not like doctors.

c20 Very few people like surgery, is that what you mean?

p20 We just do not go to doctors.

c21 Do you feel that God can sort of work through the doctors to heal you?

p21 No, God can do it by Himself

c22 Mrs. S, you seem afraid.

p22 Afraid of what, Chaplain.

c23 You tell me what you are afraid of.

p23 You mean I'm afraid of the doctors?

c24 Are you? (Head down, looking at the floor, and then she looks out the window) Are you afraid of anyone or anything?

p24 Well, I hadn't thought of that.

c25 Of what?

p25 That I'm afraid.

c26 What are you afraid of?

p26 I'm afraid of surgery.

c27 I am too. I hate to be cut on, but is that the only thing you are afraid of?

p27 Yes, I think so.

c28 How about your church members back home? What are they going to say about their pastor being in the hospital?

p28 That is a great concern for me.

c29 What will they say?

p29 We do not go to doctors.

c30 So you are concerned about what they say about you than you are your healing?

p30 I have never seen it that way, but you have a point, Chaplain.

c31 What is the point I have.

p31 I'm thinking about what people are going to say.

c32 Is God any less God to you if He uses the doctors to help in you healing?

p32 No, He is still all powerful.

c33 Yes, I would agree with you. I want to assure you that God is still God regardless of the means he uses to bring on your healing. He loves you and He is near you regardless of where you are. Hold on to your faith in God and be open to whatever he chooses to do in your life. Because you are here in need of surgery does not mean that God is failing nor that you are; He works in miraculous ways.

p33 Chaplain, that is very helpful to me. Thank you.

c34 That's good.

p34 Keep me in your prayers, Chaplain.

c35 Yes, I will. Would you like me to pray with you now?

p35 Yes, I sure would.

EVALUATION:

ANALYSIS. A worried and frightened woman who was quite concerned about what the member of her religious congregation were doing to say about her being in the hospital. I got the feeling that she had done a lot of preaching against doctors and medicine and now she was in Walter Reed for surgery for cancer. The situation was taking its toll on her emotions.

While I did not want to shatter her faith in God, felt the need to help her clarify certain understandings as to the power and love of God. I tried to let her know that the fact that she is here is no indication that God is not with her, nor that He does not love her. I did

CRITIQUE: She attempted to come across as a strong person Who had to protect her image in her church. She seemed more concerned about what others would say than about her own healing. I'm not sure I dealt with that effectively enough.

THEOLOGICAL REFLECTION: She reminded me of Nicodemus who rather than put his status and prestige in the religious community on the line, chose to visit with Jesus by night, This women is allowing her religious connection (I'm not placing a judgment on her position, just rejecting) to slow up the healing process. The fact that she is at Walter Reed Army Medical Center indicates a serious medical condition. My concern was that she takes care of her medical needs and not the needs of her congregation back home.

APPENDIX C

C. Pastoral Care Report (Mrs. S, 13 Jan 86)

Rev. Doe   Name of Patient: Mrs. S

Date of Visit: 13 Jan 86   Religion: Protestant

Number of Visits: Sex: Female

Length of Visit: Age: 58

Date of Presentation: Ward: 66

4 Feb 86

Military Status: Dependent   Wife of retired Army MSG

(A continuation of Pastoral Care Report of 7 Dec 85)

Pastoral Care Report dated 7 December 1985 was during the patient's initial visit and subsequent hospitalization at Walter Reed Army Medical Center (WRAMC). The patient has since returned to WRAMC for follow-up and evaluation of progress of the previous surgery performed over a month ago. She is now back on Ward 66 and is facing further evaluation and possibly further surgery. She has a niece who lives in the immediate area that shares the same religious faith tradition as the patient. As the chaplain for the ward I happened to recognize her face and during my visits 1 engaged her in a conversation. She expressed joy that I was yet her chaplain brit was somewhat depressed at being here and not knowing what further tests would reveal. What follows is a sequel to an earlier Pastoral Care Report and is presented to the committee because I find close similarities between her present theological stance and the theological environment in which I was reared. My struggle is that I feel that I know where she is and can identify with her position but I fell that I have grown beyond where she is now. The temptation is to "show her what is right" theologically while professionally I must allow her to be who she is and affirm her faith in God. I ask feedback as to how I got in the way of ministry, if I did, and how I might improve my ministry. I ask specific help with theological struggle. Does one deny his own theology in support of others? Can one be authentically true to his tradition while supporting others' tradition? Does one have to be any less than who he is if he affirms and supports others in their religious belief. I would like to honestly affirm and support other's faith stance and at the same time not feel guilty that I have somehow betrayed my own tradition. What I am asking for is help with increasing my ability and willingness to appreciate, validate and support the religious beliefs of others as equally valuable as my own.

VERBATIM

c37 Hello Mrs. S, how are you on today?

p37 Oh, Hi Chaplain. I'm doing okay today. I went home after my surgery and now I'm back for evaluation.

c38 Oh!

p38 Yes Chaplain. It has been a trying time for me.

c39 It has?

p39 Yes, a little rough on me since I've seen you. c40 A little rough? What does that mean to you?

p40 Chaplain, sometimes I just wonder why all of this. You live all you know to live, treat everybody right and then you come down with cancer.

c41 Seems like you have had quite a time since 1 have seen you? How about yours concerns, how are you handling all this?

p41 (She looks up at roe without saying a word, then she drops her head and a few seconds of silence follow), Chaplain, it has been rough for me.

c42 How is it for you now Mrs. S?

p42 Chaplain, I have to hold on. I have not been able to do as much as I would like to at church since I have been sick. (Her heads drops, she gets quiet for a few moments and then she looks up at me as if to ask for some answers).

c43 Mrs. S, you mentioned that you have to hold on. What does holding on mean to you now?

p43 Well, the people in the church do not know what is wrong with me. I have not told them. I really do not know myself, I just know what the doctors say.

c44 (I stand there and look at her as she looks towards the ceiling. I allow a few moments without interruption) It is not clear to me what you mean by holding on.

p44 Well, I have to hold on to my faith in God. They look up to we so much.

c45 Uh! (I remain silent for a few moments).

p45 God is using my sickness to make me stronger. You know there are some low valleys and high mountains, but He is taking me through and He is making me strong, (She looks at me and smiles slightly) so I must hold onto God.

c46 Mrs. S, it seems like you are committed to your faith and I would like you to know that I support your faith in God.

p46 Chaplain, I really do appreciate hearing that from you.

c47 You are quite welcome.

p47 It is good to know that you are not in this alone (silence, pause).

c48 Uh Huh!

p48 Sometimes I feel a little alone. But you came by when I was here before and that made me feel so good. I really feel good that you are here today. Chaplain I need your prayers. I'm going in for evaluations tomorrow, I do not know what will happen.

c49 Scary.

p49 (She drops her head as if to go into deep thought), Yes Chaplain. If I said I was not, I would not be telling the truth (Silence).

c50 So, Mrs. S it is normal for you and me to be scared when we face sickness and even death. But our faith in God as understood through Jesus Christ is our eternal hope. You, I, nor the doctors know what happen on tomorrow during your evaluation, but I want you to know that God is with you now, on tomorrow, throughout life and death and beyond this life.

That is care of the Christian faith. We have a sure hope that life's experiences are not all there is for us to believe in Jesus Christ. That is the hope that I want to share with you.

p50 So, praise God, praise God. (She goes into what appeared to be deep thought, I do not interrupt). Thank you Chaplain for helping me to better understand what I believe and preach.

c51 You are quite welcome. (I remain silent for a few moments).

p51 (She looks off and then she looks me squarely in the eye) Chaplain, it is so strange how God does things.

c52 Oh!

p52 Yes. He is working when you think not, isn't He?

p53 It may be that one of God's reasons for sending me here was to meet you.

c54 How does that make you feel?

p54 Well, just talking with you has meant so much to me. I have read the Word of God so much but there is always more to learn about God's Word.

c55 Yes, I agree with you. We are all learning more each day about God's will for us. I'm glad, that we were able to share with each other. Mrs. S, I want to assure you that He will you on tomorrow during your evaluations and in the days ahead as I have shared with you earlier.

p55. Chaplain, it helps me to hear that it does not matter or bother me to hear those words again

c56 Mrs. S, I will keep you in prayers and concerns. I will plan to visit with you later.

p56 Thank you, Chaplain. Keep me in your prayers.

c57 I will. Would you like to have prayer before I go?

p57 Oh yes!

c58 (We join hands) God our Father, I thank you today for Mrs. S. I thank you for her life of service and commitment to you and your work. I pray your blessings upon her now. Be with her now and on tomorrow during her evaluations. We pray for her family: husband, children and relatives, I pray for the members of her church back home. I pray for them understanding, patience and love. In Christ name I pray, Amen. (When I opened my eyes I noticed that she still has hers closed. I do not interrupt her and allow her to re-join me).

p58 Thank you, Chaplain.

c59 You are quite welcome. Good-bye.

p59 Good-bye, Chaplain.

EVALUATION.

ANALYSIS: This woman presented me with one of the greatest opportunities for ministry I have had in recent years. During the first PCR my concern was whether I had gotten hooked by her in the sense that her religion and position on the Bible was so close to where I was some years ago. My tendency was to move her to another level of theology. Reflecting on the initial visit now, it might have been meeting my own needs rather than her's to move her. I feel that she was moved during the second visit only because she wanted to. 1 feel that my sharing my faith with her and allowing her to share hers with me was quite facilitative.

CRITIQUE: The woman was not only wrestling with the uncertainly of the evaluations on tomorrow but with the idea of her as a preacher who had preached divine healing would herself now be in the hospital for cancer. There is the **possibility** of being branded betrayer and as one who had "lost the faith" by the members of tier church back home. She seemed to have come to some grips with that since the first visit. However, I'm not sure it is resolved yet for her. I feel that I helped her to think seriously about it.

THEOLOGICAL REFLECTIONS: While this woman had an image to **protect** back in her local church, she runs the risk of being rejected by that **church** also. The fact that she chose to come to WRAMC without letting her parishioners know where she was reminds me of Nicodemus who seeks an audience with Jesus out of the public view. But looking back on the situation I see her as coming very close to Judas the betrayer. For, in a sense, she could be seen and treated as one who had betrayed the faith and trust of her congregation. The insight for me as a theologian is that theology emerges out of the existential situation of persons and reflects where they/ he/she is at that time on the journey. The symbolism associated with that theology is **acquired** from cultural **experiences** and has validity and relevancy for the adherent. It is one thing for me to say that theoretical but it is different to make the practical application. I feel that I made a genuine effort in this second visit. I feel very good **about** the slice of ministry God did in spite of me. I am humbled that he used me at a critical time in the life of this person. I shall keep my ears and eyes open and pray that He will do it again in an even greater way. Amen.

APPENDIX D

D. Pastoral Care Report (Mr. S)

Rev. J. Doe   Religion: Protestant

Number of Visits: One   Sex: Male

Length of Visits: 20 Minutes Age: 49

Patients Name: Mr. S

NARRATIVE

While on duty on 13 March 1986, I was doing pre-ops and noticed that there was a person on Ward 55 who was scheduled for surgery on the following day. I checked the Alpha Roster to determine the religious preference of the patient and noticed he was **protestant. Du** ring the course of the evening I arrived at the ward, checked the nurses' station to determine the room in which the patient was located. After doing so, I visited the room. Upon my arrival I was informed by the patient in the next bed that the person for whom I was looking was not in the room and that he did not know his whereabouts. I thanked him for his information and asked him how was he doing. To the question, he responded, "Oh, not too good Chaplain". He had **apparently** heard me mention to the person on the other side of the room that I was Chaplain Doe, or had he recognized the name on the coat. He was lying on his back; his wife was sitting in the chair next to the bed. He had a few smiles on his face; she looked rather depressed. I picked up on their affect, which indicated a bit of despair, shock, and some fear. I was in the middle of my pre-ops and wanted rush on but decided to remain there. I sensed that they **(husband** and wife **wanted to** talk to me), had a lot on their minds and were not ready for me to leave. The wife was really expressing her feelings verbally and affectively but the **husband** (1SG) was coming **across** as calm, cool, and collected. I did not expect any other affect from him given the lifestyle he has lived for the past twenty-five years. I have found myself going to visit one patient, finding that patient out, and then end up visiting with another patient. I ask the group to look at this with me and give me feedback as to if I am doing an unfocused ministry; should 1 allow myself to be **collared** by people in the halls or should I avoid that and do ministry for those for whom I am looking? Do I need to become more intentional in ministry?

VERBATIM

c1 (I walked into the room looking for the patient whom I went to visit, I noticed that he was out of his bed. I looked over at the person in the next bed and said hello. That hello led to the conversation that resulted in the verbatim). Hello, I'm Chaplain Johnson. (He extended his hand, we shake hands).

p1 Hello, I'm 1SG. (He looks to his left), this is my wife. (She extends her hand and I shake her hand also).

c2 Hi! I'm glad to meet you, Chaplain/

p2 Hello Mrs. S, I'm glad to meet you. I came to visit Mr.? He does not seem to be here.

c3 No, he is out. Don't know where he is.

p3 Well, Thank you 1SG. How are you today?

c4 Okay Chaplain, Okay (He says that with quite bit of spirit. He re-positions himself in the bed, smiles. I thought if he is okay, what is he doing here?

p4 How long have you been a patient here?

c5 Oh! Just brought me in two days ago (He quite, looks at his wife then back at me. I just stand there and look. The fact that he and his wife looked at each other with a bit of despair).

p5 Uh! Huh! (Felt that there was more he wanted to say, but he needed to project a strange image as an old 1SG. I did not wish to rush him).

c6   Yeah. (He drops his head) I retired in 1980, after 25 years' active duty, got me another job, and was going on just fine. (He stops and looks down for a few moments), and then during a check-up, they discover I have cancer.

p6   Um! (I could pick up from this affect that lie was having a rough time with the new detected condition).

c7   Yeah! They checked out a sample of my stool and found I have rectal cancer.

p7   (When he makes that statement he and her are moved affectively, they look at each other, hold hands). Sound serious.

c8   Yeah! But I will be alright. (This is the take-charge 1SG talking, wife nods an approving yes).

p8   What does all, this mean to you all?

c9   Well, they say they think they can take care of it with radiation treatments. I should be out of here and back on the go in a few weeks or a month or so

p9   Sound pretty optimistic. (I got the feeling that he was still trying to protect his big image and was saying what his wife wanted to hear. I detected a bit of grief and wanted to help him to verbalize it if he chose to do so.

c10 Well, I hope for the best chaplain.

p10 (I look at the wife, I wanted to keep her as part of the dynamic because she was involved too). Not easy for you all.

c11 (They hold hands and at this point she is teary-eyed). No Chaplain, it is not. He has been very active. We never dreamed anything like this was wrong.

p11 Sounds like a surprise.

c12 (He cuts in) Yeah, it really was. You never know what is wrong inside of you.

p12 That was true, we never know.

c13 (His wife cuts in). He has been so active, and now this.

p13 I spent 25 years on active duty, got out, got another job, (He smiles and makes a few gestures with his hand), but I guess things are going to be a little different now.

c14 A little different now.

p14 Well, I don't know exactly how much I'll be able to do over. My concerns is, if I slow myself down (when he said that I immediately thought of myself).

c15 Yes, you might have to slow down. (He looked at me as if he was surprised I would say that).

p15 That would be a bit hard at my age. I'm not ready to retire again yet, Chaplain. (He looks at me as if to say this thing slipped up on me without warning).

c16 Well, you might have to slow down or change your lifestyle.

p16 Yeah, that possibly (I got the feeling that this was an uncomfortable subject with his wife present). I will have to wait and see what happens. Then I will make a decision.

c17 (I felt cut off and dismissed at that comment, so I chose not to push. I felt that I had raised another possibility with him). I wish you well 1SG in your stay here at the hospital.

p17 Thank you, Chaplain.

c18 You are quite welcome, good-bye.

p18 Good-bye, Chaplain.

THEOLOGICAL REFLECTIONS: I have been concerned that most of my theological reflections in some way find a close similarity to Peter. "The Big Fisherman" and am I wondering if the frequent analogy might say something of me as a person as well as it might the patient. The patient certainly did come across as one who was still in charge even with his facing cancer. He was still in the state of denial. He did not want to accept this as reality and, neither did his wife. I was not comfortable enough with him to do what I might have done as a pastor. Throughout the visit I picked up that he might have opened up had his wife not been there. But, because she was there he appeared to want to show her that he was okay.

APPENDIX E

E. Pastoral Care Report (Mr. H)

Rev. Doe   Religion: Protestant

Number of Visits: One   Sex: Male

Length of Visits: 30 Minutes Age: 66

Patients Name: Mr. H

NARRATIVE

Upon entering Ward 66, I visited with a patient whom I notice was protestant as a result of patient's cards at the nurse's station. Upon entering the room, I noticed that the patient was alone in a 4-bed room. It appeared that the other patients had recently been in the room but were perhaps out for appointments, etc. The room was well lighted but no cards, flowers or books. The patient was lying on his back looking up at the ceiling but turned toward me when he appeared to have heard footsteps. The patient took a deep thought and his facial expressions indicated worry. I ask for feedbacks as to what I might have done better or more effectively.

VERBATIM

c1 Good Afternoon. I'm Chaplain Doe.

p1 Hello, Chaplain.

c2 How are you today?

p2 Well, not too good Chaplain. I'm a little worried.

c3 Uh!

p3 Well, they are running tests and I will just have to wait and see what happens.

c4 Worried?

p4 Yes, Chaplain, I am. It's hard to just wait.

c5 Just wait.

p5 Uh! Huh! Well I would rather know now. I'll just wait and see.

c6 Some concerns.

p6 Yes I do, Chaplain. I thought I had my life all planned and now this

c7 Life all planned?

p7 Well, I do not know what to expect yet.

c8 Hard on you'?

p8 Yes, I do have some deep concerns. But, I could be wrong.

c9 Could be wrong?

p9 The test results.

c10 What do you expect?

p10 I would hope they are negative.

c11 I would join you in that hope.

p11 Well, I'm a reservist, I have a good job as a civilian and I was just planning on a good future. There are a lot questions that I do not have answers to.

c12 Questions?

p12 Chaplain I am religious. I am a Christian. Why is all of this happening to me? I just do not understand.

c13 Why is it happening to you?

p13 Yes. I pray and ask God to forgive me, but I do not know if he has forgiven me.

c14 Forgiven

p14 (Head down for a while and then he looks up at me). I just want to know that I am forgiven. I have sinned.

c15 We all have, are you willing to accept God's forgiveness.

p15 Yes, Chaplain, I am.

c16 Then why don't you? Did you ever think that God has forgiven you already but that you have not accepted it?

p16 Is it all I need to do is accept God's forgiveness?

c17 Yes!

p17 Chaplain (He looks me in the eyes) I feel so much better now. I can face my tests results more positively now.

c18 Feel better about forgiveness and the test results.

p18 Both, Chaplain, Both. Chaplain, pray for me.

c19 Would you like me to pray with you now?

p19 Yes, Chaplain.

c20 (My hands on his shoulders, the doctor and nurse walk in but notice that I am praying and they quietly leave the room). God our Father, I thank you for forgiving the sins of Mr. H. Let him know that you love him and care for him in spite of what happens in life. Might you continue to be with him in the days ahead. In Christ's name, Amen.

p20 Thank you, Chaplain.

c21 You are quite welcome. I will plan to get back to visit you again.

p21 Ok, Chaplain. I would love that.

c22 Good-bye.

p22 Good-bye Chaplain.

EVALUATION:

ANALYSIS: The patient first appeared to me to be asleep, brit, I later learned that he was just lying in a relaxed position. He seemed very worried and declined to discuss the test results that were due in a few days.

CRITIQUE: The visit went quite well I was not happy with refusal to discuss this condition but I respected la is right to refuse. He seemed to have been on a guilt trip due to something in his past. I did not force him to discuss whatever that might have been, my concern was to be with him and assure him of God's love and care.

THEOLOGICAL REFLECTION: Here was a man who seemed to feel that lie was being cost off from life while yet young. He wanted to confess his sins and I came along just in time while he was alone in the room and he took the time to confess sins in general. He reminds me of Zacchaeus who upon meeting Jesus, quickly confessed his sins and offered to make restitution. I tried to assure him God's forgiveness and he confessed that he accepted it.

CHAPTER III

BIBLICAL PERSPECTIVES OF PERSONAL HEALING

1. Old Testament Perspectives

With this topic in mind, Biblical Perspectives of Personal Healing, I shall use as my point of departure the Old Testament and explore several concepts which relate to personal healing as were espoused and believed by Old Testament writers. This study will inevitably and unavoidably force us to examine certain aspects of Hebraic theology as an attempt to ascertain the importance of personal healing during the Old Testament era. Because a number of the earliest Christians where really people who came from and were inherently a part of that Old Testament Hebraic religion, much of what we will see in the later New Testament development will, in a sense, reflect Hebrew culture and concepts. Therefore, it is necessary to explore the New Testament basis and concept of personal healing as espoused first by the Jesus of history and perpetuated by the first-century Christian community, both in Palestine and in the Hellenistic world of Paul's day. Personal healing will include wholistic healing: the healing of the mind, body, and spirit. A basic presupposition is that God is concerned about the whole person and not just a fragmented part of the person.

When one talks about healing there immediately appears on the mental horizon the presupposition that a disease or diseases are present. A disease in terms of medical and physiological definitions is a physiological degeneration of, or a morbid change in the bodily tissues, the perversion of body or mind. Medical evidence shows that pathogenic organisms are parasitic in composition. Therefore, a disease may be defined as a product of relationships between associated organism in which one exhibits functional or structural degeneration from the norm because of the activities of another. Among the ancient pathological concepts of disease was the idea that the gods had visited upon them these diseases because of certain violations of taboos, laws, or religious codes. Ancient and nomadic, and tribal Israel emerged from that kind of cultural environment arid therefore they inevitably adopted and adapted to many of the cultural norms of the larger societies.

In philosophy there is a term we call eclecticism which means that one has before him or her a large number of choices; eclecticism means that one reaches into those choices and selects the one that is more appropriate and usable by that person. So while Israel did select many concepts and ideas from the larger society, Israel realized that the basis on which her whole livelihood as a nation and as a people was upon the God of Abraham, Isaac, and Moses. Israel was extremely eclectic. When we deal with this business of sickness and healing, as far back as the book of Job, there was the idea of sickness, sin, and healing. However, the theologies of a number of the biblical writers suggest that diseases were sent by God to punish for transgressions, or an expression of God's wrath, as in Exodus 4:11 and Deuteronomy 32:39. Obviously, this concept did not originate with those who composed the Levitical (Leviticus 13) and Deutoronomistic codes. For as far back as the Book of

Job, which is probably one of the oldest books in the Bible, we have present in that writer's theology the idea that sickness is the work of the adversary or sin. So the prevailing idea in the Book of Job is that the righteous do not suffer, only the sinful. Theodicy is that theological concept used to **somehow** defend and support the goodness, the righteousness, the justice of God in the world, in the light of present evil. The great question is how can you believe and prove that God is all-powerful, all-knowing, and all-wise when the world seems to be running out of control as a runaway wagon? Perhaps, that was a question of their day and is essentially a question today. The concern, one should think, is also a question of primary importance in our day because of the colossal military situation, the economic imbalance, and the social injustices. This day of moral decay and spiritual decline will also force us to raise that question subconsciously. How can God be the God with all power and the world seems to be running out of control? One might do well to notice that neither did the Hebrews understand all of these questions and they did not have answers. It is in that sense that the Bible is a statement of faith rather than a scientific product. Thus, the Bible does not purpose to be an in-depth treatment of how heavenly bodies go; but for the faith community, it is believed that therein is contained insights as to the key to eternity with the creator.

Israel raised those questions and one can very well and very easily identify with their raising of those questions because Israel believed that the universe was theocentric, weaning that God is the central interest and ultimate concern and that the government under which they lived was theocratic which means God is in charge. If God is in charge, why are things running out of control?

Healing may be described as the curing or restoring to health of a sick person. This may include promoting the closing of a wound, the repairing of a broken limb as the result of an accident or surgical due to disease. It may involve the administering of effective treatments to deal with that pathological condition of not only the body but the mind. Health is the absence of disease. A person is healthy when that person is able to perform all the proper functions of the body and mind. In First Samuel 16:18 the reference to David's stature suggests that health was regarded as the greatest of all earthly benedictions. Total health refers to the totally healed person. It seems to me that we sometimes fail when we deal with a person as a fragmented person and deal with persons as a dichotomy and dissect the person, and cut the person up into several parts and focus only on the person's spiritual needs and do not tend to focus on the body and mind. I think that Jesus so vividly and so eloquently and so pointedly said in the text today that the person is a tin it. Man is a person; humankind are persons that are made up of several parts. And if you are going to deal with humankind's soul then you are going to have to deal with the social order in which the persons live out their lives and realize individual destinies.

Within the confines of Old Testament Judaism, medicine and physicians are held in high esteem. From earliest biblical time, the Kohanim (priest) were custodians of public health, wardens in charge of social-hygiene regulation that feature very prominently in the Levitical code. Approximately six hundred thirteen (613) biblical commandments are mentioned as hygienic in nature. These include prevention of epidemics, suppression of venereal diseases, frequent washings, care of the skin, and strict sanitary and quarantine provisions. Contagion was prevented by following detailed rules of precautionary isolation, burning or scalding of infected garments and utensils, and a thorough inspection and purification of the diseased person after recovery. It can be rightly posited that hygienic and ritual purity health and medicine are very much a part of the Jewish tradition. In the Mishnah and the Germarra which make up to the Jewish Talmud is found the same health and medical preoccupation as found in the Old Testament.

The major focus on the Talmud is on the prevention of disease and the care and health of the community. A typical admonition in the Talmud is "Bodily cleanliness leads to spiritual cleanliness." This is perhaps the basis of the old adage: *Cleanliness is next to godliness."

The task of enforcing the Old Testament and Talmudic hygienic laws rested with the Rabbis. Therefore, they had to become experts on both human and animal anatomy and pathology. Health and freedom from disease was very much a part of Old Testament concern. Based upon the Old Testament, it is quite obvious that Jewish dietary laws on kosher and now-kosher foods have a direct interest in health and medicine. In a number of Old Testament references these requirements have been spiritualized, but nonetheless, there is evident the aspect of, and interest in a whole and healthy body. Much of Hebrew theology and its perspectives a health emerged out of the present situations of their day. Because the Jews were basically agricultural in occupation, weaklings could not stand up to the day-to-day demands of a nomadic, shepherding, agrarian society. The ideal person was physique and robust, and weak lings and invalids constituted a societal problem. There were laws to protect the weak, the halt, the blind, brit society made it difficult for anyone who was not in full possession of their faculties.

The Hebrew community felt so strongly about health that there was included in the Torah the privilege of setting aside the Torah to protect life and health. Rabbi Simon Ben Menassia said, "We are told, You shall keep the Sabbath, for it is holy unto you." (Exodus 31:13). But he went on to say: "...that means that the Sabbath is given over to you, but you are not given over to the Sabbath." Rabbi Nathan says, "The people of Israel shall keep the Sabbath, to observe it through generations." (Exodus 31:16). "That means it is alright to violate one Sabbath in order to keep many Sabbaths afterwards." Rabbi Yehudad says, "We are to keep the commandments, which if a man do them he will live by them." (Leviticus 18:5). "That means, live by them to ensure health and wholeness, however, violate the law if by so doing you will live many more years to come." In other words, ".... if your ox is in the ditch on the Sabbath and is about to die and if he dies you are not going to live for many more Sabbaths, then you take the ox out of the ditch." This position suggests that there is inherent the possibility of on-coming futuristic situations and conditions imperceptible by both medicine and religion of their day. Therefore, they allow the latitude for what might be called existential appropriation, or application when those events and situations occur. What is said here is that a possible threat to live sets aside the Sabbath laws.

The health of the patient is supreme in Old Testament thought. If a person feels sick and the doctor says he is well, you obey the sick person; if the doctor says the person is sick and the person says lie is well, you obey the doctor. It is safe to say that all laws of the Torah are suspended on the possibility that life is in danger. If the military is attacking you on the Sabbath, why sit around in the Church and say we will get him first thing in the morning when buildings are falling in on you. I think this is a theological statement made here. It simply suggests to me that the Old Testament writers and Rabbis knew that there would come a day in the future whose situations and conditions were really imperceptible to them of that day, so they included into the law certain flexibilities which gave them the latitude to deal with futuristic situations and conditions that would allow them to sort of do what philosophers call make it existential, or to apply it right on the scene or give meaning to it right then and there. What is said is that the possible threat to live sets aside the Sabbath

The possible threat to life means setting aside the Sabbath law. The Sabbath was made for man and not man for the Sabbath, therefore man has the flexibility to somehow become Lord of the Sabbath in the Old Testament. That is almost a direct quote of Jesus Himself.

Healthy bodies and longevity were prized possessions in antiquity. The Hebrews thought of health in terms of physical strength and well-being. Mental or emotional disturbances were generally related to some specific organ of body. The Hebrew word shalom, which means healthy or whole which is a complement of the Hebrew word shalom which means peace. Length of days and long life were the ideal but if a man lived beyond the three score and ten years as is seen as a normal life expectancy in Psalms 90:10, then hardships and sorrow were to be expected as a logical outcome. Genesis 6:3 states that a man's life span was one hundred twenty (120) years, and this was the age attained by Moses. It was customary to recognize a long and prosperous life by saying a man lived one hundred ten (110) years and this is the age ascribed to Joseph in Genesis 50:26. It seems evident that longevity was a prized possession, an ultimate goal in the ancient world and that maintaining a clean and healthy body and mind contributed to the process.

The Hebrews held to a communal concept, or to a sense of community that what effects one affects all. They displayed the concept that no one person is what one ought to be until all have been given the chance to become what they ought to be. In fact, I feel very strongly that this is what Emmanuel Kant has in mind when he formulates the Categorical imperative where he talks about oughtness. This is evident when you look around the world you see that the real is loot necessarily the ought. One might easily see that there is possibly something wrong in our world that suggests that a significant number of our problems might stem from the fact that we are too individualistic and that we leave very little sense of community. Numerous situations in our society lead one to conclude that there is the inclination that '... if I make it as an individual everything is alright." This is nowhere more evident than at traffic signals, check-out counter, and at voting lines. But I feel very strongly that the human family is somehow interrelated! We are interconnected! We are intertwined! We are interwoven! And we are inextricably bound up together so that what affects me individually affects the whole of humankind collectively. Each of us ought not to be just concerned about our own self-growth and development. We ought to expand our theological, cultural and social horizons so that they can include the totality of human existence. We love everybody in the world as American Christians! We love every Chinese in China, as long as they stay in China. We love every African in Africa, as long as they stay in Africa. By the same token, we love every drug addict, pimp, prostitute, and bum in the streets, as long as they stay where they are: the problem arises when they move next door to us. Historically, our society is rather reluctant to gravitate towards and accept persons who are different front us. Sadly, this reluctance penetrates the whole of our society.

Now as I said earlier, dealing and health were of primary importance in the Old Testament, healing in the Old Testament takes on a spiritualized significance. Healing in the Old Testament, while sickness is used ninety-eight percent (98%) of the time, sickness and healing as used in the Old Testament also has a spiritualized meaning. In other words, I have wounded and I will heal. That is a highly spiritualized view and treatment of the understanding of healing. If you will obey my laws. "God says to Moses to tell Israel coming out of Egypt.

If you keep my commandments, I will not put on you the diseases that I put on the Egyptians." That is a direct reference to pathological or physiological sickness. When we come to II Chronicles 7:14 which has served for many as a number one text for revival God's promise of health is very significant. That reference there is not necessarily a physical malady or physical sickness. When we come to Job we find another situation where there is a totally different concept of sickness because it was a part of the wisdom literature of Job's day that only bad folk suffered.

We still have a lot of folks who believed that today, and will even raise the question, either individually or openly, my God she/he has been in the church all of these years and she/he is going through all of this? What happened in her/his life somewhere that is causing all of this to happen? This seems to be the prevailing questions in the minds of Job's friends who came to see him. There are people who still feel that sickness is tantamount to sin. The eternal message of the Book of Job says that number one, you don't know the answer, and that much of the time during your answer-giving, you are merely beating in the dark. In fact, Job said, "I don't know the answer." We just don't have the answers to all of our plaguing questions, even today.

Most of the references to healing from Genesis to the close of the Old Testament Canon have to do with spiritual sickness and spiritual healing. Not that physical sickness was denied by Old Testament persons, but because they understood that sickness was due to sin, the admonition is heavily inclined toward spiritual correction. II Chronicles 7:14 is a specific reference to a divinely mandated spiritual repentance as a condition for the healing of the agricultural economy of the nation. The belief was that spiritual correction was the answer to physical malady, II Chronicles 32:24-26 and Isaiah 39:1-2. The three most dreaded diseases in the Old Testament world were leprosy, blindness, and deafness: Exodus 4:11; Leviticus 13; and II Kings 6:18. The earliest Old Testament reference to health and healing is Genesis 43:28, where Joseph's brothers replied to his question as to Jacob's health. The reference to his life was chronological and physical life, the implication that Jacob's physical body was minus diseases, and needed no healing in the pathological sense. Exodus 15:26, on the other hand, "I am the Lord that healeth thee," is a condition placed upon Israel that if they would adhere to God's laws, that He (God) would not put the diseases upon them that He put on the Egyptians. This is a direct reference to physical healing or the prevention of sickness itself. But in Deuteronomy 32:39, "I wound and I deal," is a theological statement attesting to the ethical monotheism, omnipotence, and to the omnipresence of Israel's God. II Kings 2:22 is to prove God's wholistic approach to human needs: He not only heals persons; He heals their environment.

II Kings 20:5-1 I attest to God's authority over the physical sickness in the body of Hezekiah and further suggest the power of prayer in causing God to alter conditions and situations. Except for the brief reference to healing, Psalms 103:3-4; Isaiah 53:5, Old Testament references to healing are of the soteriological, salvific, messianic, and eschatological Nature. It seems safe to posit that past example upon the frequent figurative references in the Bible to sickness, diseases, and healing, that these were real problems and threats to the well-being of life. It was characteristic of Old Testament theology to project into the future those questions to which no immediate answer was available. This is most vividly see in the Old Testament shift from messianism to apocalypticism toward the close of the Old Testament Canon.

2. New Testament Perspectives

Then we come to the New Testament where Jesus is the great physician. In fact, Mark is very harsh on doctors perhaps because he is not a part of the medical profession. He says that the woman with the issue of blood had suffered many things because of physicians. She had spent all of her money from doctor to doctor. Instead of getting better, she kept getting worse, which seems to be a put down of the medical profession. Then Luke gives a more perfect understanding of the incident. That's what he says in the first chapter of Luke. Luke explains that the woman had spent all of her money and wasn't getting better, but then Jesus came by the Situation changed. To some, this might sound like a doctor looking out for his profession.

Perhaps the most important verses in the Bible are verses 1-2 of Isaiah 61, and the slight change in Luke's presentation of Jesus' quotation of those verses in St. Lake 4:18-19: "The spirit of the Lord is upon me... to heal the brokenhearted, to preach deliverance to the captives... the recovering of sight to the blind, to set at liberty them that are bruises." These verses have become the rallying cry of a number of feminist and liberation theologians since the development of modern-day Black Theology. Belt a close examination of the verses suggests a wholistic approach to the human predicament. These verses, both in Isaiah and in Luke, see the person as a unity whose healing cannot be dichotomous Therefore, true healing must include the total person.

Luke's Messiah was to preach the Gospel to the poor and as a result of that preaching, broken hearts would be mended, captives would be delivered, sight to the blind would be resorted and the bruised would be liberated. One must raise the historical and theological question that is obviously present in Isaiah and in Luke's quotation of Isaiah. Was Isaiah's prophecy a spiritualized hope and Luke's presentation a theological interpretation? Luke, still using figurative language: brokenhearted is spiritualized, and is a physiological impossibility. The only physiological aspect of Luke's message is the recovering of sight to the blind. The bulk of the references to healing in the New Testament are references to physical healing. St. Mark, which is the first written Gospel in a chronological sense, commences the life of Jesus as one with the power to heal and to perform miracles, immediately following the baptism, he casts out demons, Mark 1:21 -25; heals Peter's mother-in-law, I:29-31; heals many sick and diseased persons, 1:32-34; and 2:1-12; in 3:1-5, he heals on the Sabbath; and in 3:6-12, he heals many others, to include those with unclean spirits.

The healing profession was held in high respect in Jesus' day and twice in the Gospels Jesus refers to Himself as a physician or healer, Mark 2:27 and in Luke 4:23. Mark seems to be the only New Testament writer who held the medical **profession** in disrespect. In Mark 5:26: "... and had suffered many things of many physicians, and had spent all that she had, and was no better, but rather grew worse..." This was his personal assessment of the medical profession. But Luke, a member of the medical profession, simply accentuates the power of Jesus to heal. In fact, Matthew captures the essence of Jesus' ministry in his worldwide perspective on mission. For Matthew, Jesus' ministry transcends racial, cultural, religious, and political barriers. Matthew 10:8 records "... heal the sick, cleanse the lepers, raise the dead, cast out demons...", is all to be done by the power given to the disciples by the Jesus of history in Matthew 10:1.

Jesus was concerned about the healing or making whole, or restoration of the total person, to include the body, mind, and soul. At some points, Jesus fits into Old Testament tradition as far as the importance of healing is concerned. But while there is a high degree of spiritualization of sickness in the Old Testament, Jesus sees sickness as a malfunction of human physiology and lack of mental balance. Jesus saw a significant interaction between psyche and soma, or mind and body. Therefore, for Jesus healing was not either-or but both and the same. This is also true of Jesus' perception of social healing. He was very much aware that social healing must include the social order in which one lives.

A. The Healing of the Body, Soul, and Mind

Mark begins his Gospel with Jesus' healings lasting for twenty-four hours of non-stop healings, Mark 1:21- 34. Healings are so important in Mark that Jess s nor his disciples can take a break and eat. Mark shows us in 1:21; 2:1-12, five examples of personal healings. In Mark 1:21- 26, the first is a demoniac who displayed or had undesirable emotions. These demons had altered his behavior while he attended church. While in Church during the worship, the unclean spirits cried out and recognized Jesus as the Son of God. Only after Jesus had rebuked him, ordered him out, do we hear the words, "He came out of him", the man. He came out of him is a medical pronouncement which means "healed" for Mark. In 1:13, Peter's mother-in-law is healed of a fever. The words "she muttered unto them..." is Mark's way of saying she had received personal healing. In Mark 1:39, "... and He casts out demons", is not only Mark's recognition of the evil power in the world that controls man but also his assertion of the power over leprosy, a most dreaded disease of the Old Testament and New Testaments. The paralytic in Mark 2:1-12, is an example of each person's responsibility to assist the sick and the feeble in their efforts to find healing. The man was brought to Jesus by the help of four men, but the verses say that "When Jesus saw their faith (the four news's faith), He said unto the sick of the palsy, son, thy sins are forgiven thee." This does not imply that Jesus saw sickness as a direct result of sin but that the man had a double problem, spiritual sin and physiological palsy. Therefore, he became free of sin and regained his equilibrium and flexibility.

I feel very strongly that sickness, in whatever form, affects the total human being. Sickness calls for readjustments, reorientation of priorities, establishing new relationships, and acceptance of the sickness itself.

Sickness fragments demoralize (as AIDS does, and TB used to do) and set you apart as an object that is less than.

B. The Healing Process

When I was a Clinical Pastoral Education strident at Walter Reed Army Medical Center, the question that always came up during small group presentations was the "how to' question. How-to implies techniques, procedures, the right words, behavior, etc. But there is no general, all-time and situation-applicable set of words: "the right techniques, procedures, words, behavior, etc." However, as medical doctors have at their disposal a number of techniques and procedures that are a part of their time-honored traditions and they still lose patients (or do they?) to death. As ministers of the Word of God and the Sacraments, we are also a part of the dealing and helping professions. We are in the business of caring for souls, bodies, and minds. There must always be present within us the belief that we have something to offer that no other profession has: we have the healing power of God in us and at our disposal. As far as techniques are concerned, let's look at a technique employed by Peter and John at the Gate Beautiful in the Acts of the Apostles.

Peter and John went up to the temple at the hour of prayer. Each day they went they saw the same man lying there with the same cup, with the same speech, "help the cripple, help the cripple, help the cripple." The cripple is not even alert, lie makes the same plea, the same monotone. He had even been helped by someone, otherwise, he would have lost faith in hand-outs but he had not received enough to fold up and go home and retire. But one-day Peter and John came by on their way to worship. Others had come by but they were possibly too busy going to church until they apparently had overlooked a key aspect of the business of the church. But Peter and Job n challenged him for the first time in his life: "Look on us."

The man's attention was downcast, but hearing Peter, he looked up expecting to receive something, money of course. Then Peter startled him by telling him what he did not have: "Silver and gold 1 have none." What a new response to the beggar's request. "But such as I have I give to thee..." And he took him by the hand, lifted him up and the man, leaping, stood up and walked. We have known for a long time the power of touch, of embrace, and of support. Others had merely thrown things to him but Peter went to him, and not just touched him, lie took him and lifted him up, up to a to new levels of reality, power, self-worth, dignity, and somebodiness. The words "rise up and walk" are shock, empathetic commands. This is what psychologists say should be done. Shock releases dormant energy in us or to receive that power from another. "There is a power that worketh in us by which God is able to do exceedingly above what we can ask or hope for."

The cure of our physical, mental, emotional, and spiritual selves lies not simply in God, nor in persons; it lies in God and persons forming an enterprise in which God and persons are working together to rid our world of physical, emotional, economic, social, and racial diseases that render persons less than the creatures God made them to be. There are certain things persons cannot do; there are certain things God will not do, but God and His human creation working together can bring wholeness, healing and health to the body, soul, and mind.

The healing and Restoring Spirit, the liberating Spirit helps one to understand an aspect of genuine, authentic ministry that might even transcend the practicum and small group settings. It is significant that in order to be a serious caregiver, one must be the best and most concerned person one knows how to be. With that quality, spiritual and academic, you will not only learn to "do", but you will learn to "be."

BIBLIOGRAPHY

Bultmann, Rudolph, <u>The Theology of the New Testament</u>, New York, Charles Scribners' Sons, 1955.

Clebsch, William A., and Jackie, Charles R., <u>Pastoral Care in Historical Perspective</u>, New York, Harper and Row, 1967.

Cone James, <u>A Black Theology of Liberation</u> New York, J.B. Lippencott Co., 1976.

Eaton, Clement, <u>The Freedom-of Thought Struggle in the Old South.</u> New York, Harper and Row, 1964.

Eichrodt, Walter T, <u>Theology of the Old Testament</u>, Vol 11 Trans by J.A. Baker, Philadelphia, The Westminster Press, 1967.

Ferder, Fran, <u>Word Made Flesh</u>, Notre Dame, Ava Maria Press, 1986.

Glasser, William, <u>Stations of the Mind</u>, Philadelphia, Harper and Row, 1981,

Hayes, John H., Introduction to the Bible, Philadelphia, The Westminster Press, 1976.

Heschel, Abraham, The Sabbath, New York, Farrar, Straus and Girous, 1978.

Hiltner, Seward, Theological Dynamics, Nashville, Abingdon Press, 1972.

Jones, Major J., Christian Ethics for Black Theology, Nashville, 1974.

Macquarrie, John, Principles of Christian Theology, New York, Charles Scribners' Sons, 1966.

Niebuhr H. Richard, Christ, and Culture, New York, Harper and Row, 1951.

Rogers, Carl. Carl Rogers on Encounter Groups, New York, Harper and Row, 1970.

Tillich, Paul, Systematic Theology, Vol 1., Chicago, The University of Chicago Press, 1951.

Woodson, Carter Godwin, The Negro in Our History, Washington, D.C., The Associated Publishers, Inc., 1922.